Organize Your Office: A Small Business Survival Guide to Managing Records

Teri J. Mark, CRM

ARMA International

Lenexa, Kansas

To Bill, my biggest fan, for his unwavering support, from beginning to end.

Consulting Editor: Mary L. Ginn, Ph.D.
Designer/Compositor: Rebecca Gray Design
Cover Art: Jason Vannatta

ARMA International
13725 West 109th Street, Suite 101
Lenexa, KS 66215
913.341.3808

ISBN: 1-931786-10-0

Printed in the United States of America.

Acknowledgments

Thank you to the ARMA publication staff, specifically Diane Carlisle and Vicki Wiler, who envisioned this book and made it happen. My thanks also to the editorial board members for their tactful suggestions and insight into making everything right.

My sincere thank you to those members of the Institute of Certified Records Managers' Exam Development Committee with whom I had the privilege of serving in the 1990s. They are the very best and the brightest in our field, including, but not limited to, Jan Hart, Dave Goodman, Mary Robek, Patrick Queen, and Laura Thomforde. They taught me more about records management than I ever could have learned in any classroom. Plus, they are a fun group, especially when it comes to margaritas.

I would also like to acknowledge my clients; specifically, Randy Kembel and Jane Owens, who recognized the value of records management in their organizations. To them I am forever appreciative of the opportunities they granted to implement all of my records management knowledge.

Thank you to Jacque Ewing-Taylor for reading and editing the first draft of the manuscript. Her willingness to share her time and her perspective were very much appreciated.

Thank you to the reference staff of the Nevada State Library and Archives, who helped research statistics.

Thank you to my mother, Kay, who always wondered what I would do with a degree in anthropology; to my big sisters, Sharon, Ellen, and Kathy, for their encouragement and support; and to my sister-in-law, Pat Grant, who turned into my second biggest fan! Thank you to my dear friends, Alice, Darla, Jacque, Kathy, Kim, and Martha, who listened to me and kept me grounded throughout this project. Last, but not least, thank you to my family, Bill, John, and Meghan, for their patience and understanding while I worked on this project.

Contents

Chapter 7   **Storage Solutions**   **43**

Chapter 8   **Filing Supply Solutions**   **54**

Chapter 9   **Making the Change to a New Filing System**   **65**

Introduction

- *Is your desk continually stacked with papers and documents?*
- *Do you meet with clients or colleagues outside your office because you are too embarrassed to have them see your cluttered office space?*
- *Are your file cabinets so overstuffed with older papers and documents that no space is available for new materials?*
- *Do you frequently ask clients or colleagues to resend information because you do not know where your information is located?*

Organize Your Office: A Small Business Survival Guide to Managing Records is directed toward the 24 million small businesses in the United States. It is specifically geared to small enterprises with fewer than 20 employees, home-based businesses, and self-employed individuals with no employees.

Many books on records management, written by records managers for records managers are available. These books present records management issues from the practitioner's perspective. They are textbooks that instruct the practitioner on the theory and methodology for developing a records management program. Some of these books may be too complex for the average businessperson who wants simple guidelines on how to organize and manage his or her business records.

Professional organizers have created a small cottage industry around organizing households, and some even delve into business and personal papers. Although their intent is correct, a professional records manager is responsible for taking it one step further. Professional organizers do an excellent job of explaining how to create efficient work habits, prioritize work time, and set up individual workspace. After that work is completed, a professional records manager needs to step in to explain to the entrepreneur how to organize and manage business records.

This book is for small business owners and managers who want to get organized and to design a records management plan for their records. The intent is not to provide an all-encompassing plan, but to provide you with enough ideas to get you on your way. Although paper records are addressed in detail, electronic records are not ignored. They are very important to small businesses.

When you organize your records, you initiate the first rule of records management: getting the right record to the right person at the right time.

Organizing Business Records

When you organize your records, you initiate the first rule of records management: getting the right record to the right person at the right time. You are setting up a filing system with the key goal of quick retrieval of the desired record.

How long, on average, do you take to retrieve a document or a file? If a valued customer is on the telephone asking questions, do you need more than 15 seconds to pull the record? If so, you may have a problem. The more time you take to fumble around in your office or computer searching for a record, the more credibility you lose.

Managing Business Records

After the records are organized, they must be managed on an ongoing basis. How does managing differ from organizing? Organizing is putting your records into an arrangement and location that will enhance their accessibility. Managing is setting up routines to make sure the records stay organized.

As much as you would like, you cannot set up a filing system and expect it to stay organized without some effort. The system requires regular routines to keep it organized. These routines include well-defined criteria for determining which records to keep and which records to toss.

Protecting Your Business

Organizing and managing your business records have other benefits as well. Disorganization and mismanagement of records can give the impression, however mistaken, to outside parties that you are selectively retaining or selectively destroying records. Governmental agencies become particularly apprehensive of businesses that keep some records but cannot produce others. In case of litigation, inconsistencies in your recordkeeping practices can prevent you from adequately protecting your business against any adverse action. Businesses, large and small, have a responsibility to protect their business records.

Small Businesses Are Booming!

Economic factors over the last decade, such as an improved economy and the increasing availability of small business loans, have contributed to the growth of small businesses. On the other hand, the recent declining economy and job layoffs have prompted others to start their own businesses. In addition, the following technological advances have played a significant role in paving the way for small business development:

- Inexpensive, quality computers and computer peripherals, such as printers and scanners, have made a small business start-up easier.
- Easy-to-use productivity software programs, such as word processing, spreadsheets, bookkeeping, desktop publishing, and contact management, permit the small business owner to accomplish many functions that previously required specialized staffing and expertise.
- Accessible, high-quality network and telecommunication systems improve internal and external communications. These systems put the small business on a competitive balance with big business. The Internet and e-mail opened the world. They allow even the smallest business leverage to do business with anyone in any location.
- Service companies, such as Kinko's™, MAIL BOXES ETC.®, and Office Depot®, have enabled a professional look for small and home-based businesses. These stores are convenient and offer an abundant array of services and products to produce a presentation that can rival the output of any big business.

Although these products and services contributed to the growth of small businesses, they have also inundated them with data. Small business owners now have more information at their fingertips than they could have possibly imagined twenty years ago. Consequently, finding ways to organize and manage this information is more important than ever.

Numerous resources are available for small business owners. Bookstores and libraries are bulging with books on small business management. The Internet is a phenomenal resource for information on business management. Small business organizations and vendors provide free access to information on business start-up and management. Universities, colleges, and business schools offer numerous courses on small business management. The U.S. Small Business Administration (SBA) provides financial, technical, and management assistance to small businesses.

In all this wealth of information, one area is consistently undervalued: How to organize and manage business records. This book will help small business owners overcome that deficiency. Additional resources are listed in Appendix 6.

Chapter 1

Why Records Management?

The basic objectives in records management are to manage and organize business records. These objectives are either misunderstood by many small business owners or dismissed as something that only large corporations can afford to do. The reality is that all companies, from the home office to the mega-corporation, benefit, both financially and productively, from records management.

What Are Records?

Records include all documents that a business creates and receives in the course of doing business.

A **record** is recorded information, regardless of medium or characteristics, made or received by an organization that is evidence of its operation and that has value requiring retention for a specific period of time.

Records arise from actual happenings; they are a snapshot of an action or event. They offer a picture of something that happened. To serve their purpose in providing reliable evidence, records in both paper and electronic form must be accurate, complete, and comprehensive.

Records Life Cycle

Surprisingly enough, records do not have eternal life. They are created, used, and stored; then they must be retired. This process is known as the *life cycle of a record*. The **records life cycle** is the life span of a record from its creation or receipt, through its useful life to its final disposition or retention as a historical record. A record moves through five phases: creation, distribution, use, maintenance, and final disposition. After a record is created, it is distributed (sent) to the user. If the user decides to keep the record for later use, the record must be maintained—stored, retrieved, and protected. The last phase is disposition. After a predetermined period of time has elapsed, records to be kept are transferred to less expensive storage. At the end of a specified number of years, the records are disposed of—destroyed or transferred to permanent storage.[1] The application of the life cycle concept, illustrated in Figure 1.1, is the foundation of records management. When a record's usefulness ends, the record should be retired or disposed of. Moving retired records out of the office makes room for active records. **Active records** are those records needed to perform current operations. They are subject to frequent use and are usually located near the user. They can be accessed manually or on-line

> A record moves through five phases: creation, distribution, use, maintenance, and final disposition.

1

Figure 1.1

Records Life Cycle

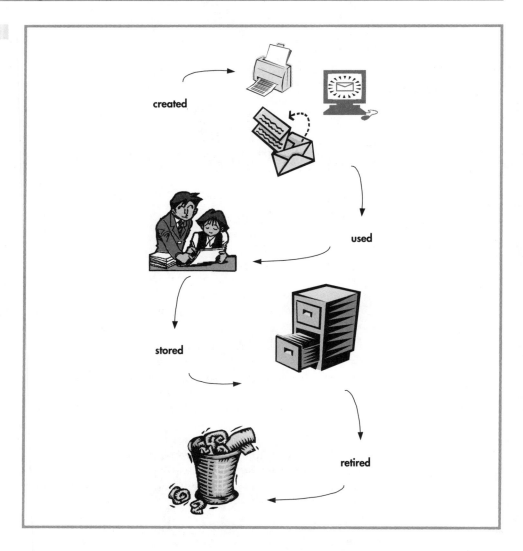

via a computer system. Records that are no longer needed for daily business should not take up valuable office space.

The key is not to turn your file cabinets into repositories for useless records. Keep recycling the space in your file cabinets so that the important records, the records that you need right now for business, are readily available. Records that have passed their usefulness should be moved out of prime office space. Transferring records will begin to make sense, once you realize that up to 90 percent of all records retrievals are for records that were created within the last three years.[2,3]

The life cycle concept applies to both paper and electronic records. Although disk storage space is relatively cheap, storing useless, inactive records on your hard drive is of no value. **Inactive records** do not have to be readily available, but they must be kept for legal, fiscal, or historical purposes. Keeping them in the same files as the active records simply slows down both you and your computer, and your backups become larger and larger. You find that even if the data exists, if you cannot find or access it, it is as good as destroyed anyway.

Records that have passed their usefulness should be moved out of prime office space.

Benefits of Records Management

A glance around your office may identify some records management problem areas. Improvements in these areas can justify an investment in a records management program. The following improvements are some of the most important ones you can achieve for your business.

- *Cost savings.* A very high percentage of business information is still paper oriented.[4,5] Filing equipment vendors estimate that storing paper records costs somewhere between $10 and $25 per filing inch.[6] In a typical office, about 90 to 95 percent of the records are nonpermanent,[7] and up to 60 percent of these records can be immediately retired, or at least moved out of the office into a low-cost storage area.[8] Emptying just one 4-drawer file cabinet can immediately save your business as much as $2,000 per year in maintenance costs.[9]

- *Improved efficiency.* Poorly organized records mean that large amounts of nonproductive time is spent searching for records. An organized filing system can improve retrieval efficiency by at least 35 percent. It can also reduce filing errors, such as misfiles and missing files, from almost 5 percent to close to zero.[10]

- *Regulatory compliance.* Many laws and regulations require some form of recordkeeping obligations, such as requiring (1) creating records, (2) reporting information to an agency, or (3) maintaining information, such as copies of reports or documents, for a specified length of time.

  For example, we are all familiar with the records creation requirements of the Internal Revenue Service (IRS) because we fill out tax forms every year. We fulfill our recordkeeping obligations, according to the IRS regulations, by (1) creating records—we fill out Form 1040, (2) reporting information—we mail Form 1040 to the IRS, and (3) maintaining information—we retain supporting documentation for Form 1040, just in case we are audited by the IRS.

  However, your business may also be obligated to comply with regulations from other U.S. federal agencies, such as the Occupational Safety and Health Administration (OSHA), the Department of Labor (DOL), and the Immigration and Naturalization Service (INS). Failure to comply with the recordkeeping regulations of these agencies may result in large fines or penalties, too.

  A good recordkeeping system will help your business stay in compliance with all regulatory agencies. Moreover, in case of an audit, if the records are accessible and properly maintained, the affects of the audit on the business are minimized.

- *Reduced litigation risk.* A poorly managed records program can leave your business vulnerable to adverse litigation action. We live in a very litigious society; any business dispute can result in litigation. Business owners must be careful to follow regular records maintenance routines so that records that must be kept can be found; and records that are no longer useful are destroyed. Do not selectively keep any records and do not selectively destroy any records. In other words, if the retention period is met on a record, throw it away. A **retention period** is the time period that records must be kept according to operational, legal, regulatory, and fiscal requirements. An exception to the retention period expiration occurs if you anticipate litigation. In this case, all potentially relevant material must be kept and not destroyed. The reasons are simple: (1) the records may contain evidence necessary to reconstruct the facts of the case that can either rebut a claim against you, or demonstrate your version of the facts; and (2) destroying any potential evidence may result in severe sanctions, including contempt of court or criminal prosecution, for obstructing justice or tampering with evidence that may be relevant to the case.

A poorly managed records program can leave your business vulnerable to adverse litigation action.

● *A feeling of well-being.* When you are organized, you will find that the office will run more smoothly. Office morale improves when employees have a pleasant place in which to work. The perception of your business to your customers and to the public will improve as well.

A disorganized office does not necessarily indicate laziness or incompetence. It is an indication that the responsible individuals may not have the necessary tools to create a well-organized records system. People are not born organizers, nor are they born filers. These processes are taught. The business owner is responsible for introducing these processes to his or her business. Effective records management can introduce a powerful competitive advantage for your business.

Notes

1. Judy Read-Smith, Mary L. Ginn, and Norman F. Kallaus, *Records Management*, 7th ed. (Cincinnati, OH: South-Western/Thomson Publishing Co., 2002), 14–15.

2. Mary F. Robek, CRM, Gerald F. Brown, and David O. Stephens, *Information and Records Management*, 4th ed. (New York: Glencoe/McGraw Hill, 1995), 63–64.

3. J. Edwin Dietel, "Draining the Corporate Records Swamp," *American Corporate Counsel Association*, 31 January 1997.

4. Ibid., *Information and Records Management*, 9.

5. Mark Langemo, Ph.D., CRM, FAI, "Filing Systems – Refinement, Development and Management," in *Proceedings of the 46th Annual ARMA International Conference in Montreal, Quebec, September 30 – October 3, 2001* (Prairie Village, KS: ARMA International, 2001).

6. Ibid.

7. Ibid., *Information and Records Management*, 61.

8. Ibid., 9.

9. Ibid.

10. Gloria Gold, CRM, *How to Set Up and Implement a Records Management System* (New York: AMACOM, 1995, out of print), 2.

Assess Your Current Filing System

You may have previously tried other processes. What aspects of those filing systems didn't work? To help you make improvements in your processes, think about what isn't working, or what failed in the past.

Many filing systems start out running smoothly, but before you know it, they turn into chaos. The good intentions were there, but the follow-through failed.

Before you can start to "fix" the problem, you have to know where you are now. Can you identify with any of the following problems?

- Too complex? Did the demands of the system overwhelm you? Some filing systems are just too complex. The system may have had too many categories, and too many ways to file a document were possible. When a new document was filed, was copying it and filing it in several places easier than spending time determining where it should be filed?

- Too simplistic? Is the system just not the right one for your records? The most common filing system is an alphabetic system. An alphabetic filing system should be no larger than a single file drawer. Any larger than that, and the system becomes too cumbersome. Because an alphabetic system is an easy system to start, many people have that type of system in their offices. The system can grow quickly, and just as quickly, get out of control. The success of the system is dependent on the file folder label. If you cannot remember how you labeled a file, you can spend too much time hunting through the files for the folder. In addition, you may have multiple files for the same correspondent. For example, you may have a file labeled *ACME Pest Control* and another file stored a few drawers away labeled *Pest Control – ACME*. See Chapter 8 for information on folder labeling.

- Held hostage? Did an employee develop a filing system so complex that only she or he understands it? The employee who designed it calls it "job security;" you call it "a nightmare." Only she or he can file, and nothing can be retrieved without that employee's assistance.

- Big desk filing? Is stacking papers on your desk, on the credenza, or on the floor easier than filing them? Some people want active records within an arm's reach, yet some of the piles have been there so long that the papers on the bottom are getting pressed into coal.

> An alphabetic filing system should be no larger than a single file drawer.

In effect, the big-desk filer holds the office hostage too, because if he or she is gone, no one can access the records. The big-desk filer sometimes may think that he or she knows exactly where a specific record is located and can quickly pull out a record. However, the reality is that most records retrievals require a lengthy search—combing and recombing through the stacks.

Do you recognize yourself in any of these situations?

Organizational Character

Are you prone to organization or disorganization? Many theories exist for why people are disorganized.

One popular theory speculates that certain personality types may point to basic preferences. To measures a person's traits and behaviors, Isabel Briggs Myers and Katharine C. Briggs developed a personality type survey, known as the *Myers-Briggs Type Indicator® (MBTI®)*. The results categorize people into four scales: (E) extraversion vs. (I) introversion, (S) sensing vs. (N) intuition, (T) thinking vs. (F) feeling, and (J) judging vs. (P) perceiving. The most organized on the MBTI is "J" (Judgmental). The J-type prefers living "a planned and organized life." For this personality type, organizing and prioritizing is a more natural trait. The opposing personality type, the "P" (Perceiver), prefers living "a spontaneous and flexible life." For this type, the personality trait is to stack and pile. A "P" personality must *want* to be organized.[1]

Another popular theory is the *Left-Brain vs. the Right-Brain*. This theory postulates that just as people are left- or right-handed, they are also left- or right-brained. Left-brain people have dominant left-brain hemispheres, while right-brain people have dominant right-brain hemispheres. The left side of the brain is logical; the right side of the brain is holistic. The left side comprehends through reasoning; the right side comprehends through images. Left-brained people think linearly, remember details, and have a good vocabulary. Right-brained people's strong points are creativity, intuition, and artistic expression. Left-brained people are organized; right-brained people are organizationally challenged.[2]

Sometimes disorganization hides an underlying problem or concern. Individuals diagnosed with attention deficit disorder (ADD) are often categorized as disorganized and cluttered. Many highly gifted and creative individuals may bear similar indicators. These individuals neither tolerate nor fit into the traditional workplace and thus aspire to be self-employed entrepreneurs. Although they are quite creative, they can also be rather organizationally challenged.[3]

On the lighter, less scientific side, you can turn to astrology to determine your organizational tendencies. Astrologists point to those born under the sign of Capricorn as the most organized. They are classified as efficient, organized, and detail-oriented. In contrast, Pisces, and, under periods of stress the occasional Gemini, can be inclined to disorganization.[4]

> An organized and well-managed records program is still one of the most effective tools in the success of your business.

Failure to Organize is Not an Option

If organizing doesn't come naturally, don't worry, you are simply part of the norm. For most people, organizing is not a natural process. The process, however, can be learned; therefore, claiming to be a right-brained thinker or a Pisces does not give you carte blanche to a disorganized work environment. An organized and well-managed records program is still one of the most effective tools in the success of your business.

Notes

1. Paul H. Pietri and Edward L. Harrison, "Personal Style in Organizational Life: Judging and Perceiving," *Industrial Management* 40 (January/February 1998), 10.

2. Mike Bourcier, "The Right-Brain Way to Manage Change," *CMA Magazine* 67, no. 5 (June 1993), 10; Jill Charles, "Performers: Yes, You are Running a Small Business," *Back Stage* 4, no. 3 (January 2000), 28.

3. Alexander J. Scholp, "Attention Deficit Disorder: Are you driven to distraction?", *Advisor Today* 96, no. 7 (July 2001), 96.

4. Shari Caudron, "Your Corporate Horoscope," *Industry Week* 247, no. 6, 16 March 1998, 64; J. T. Ford, *Zodiac Manager* (Franklin Lakes, NJ: New Age Books, 2001).

Chapter 3

Examining the Situation—
The Inventory

Now that you have made the commitment to organize, you are ready to push up your sleeves, pull out the trash bags, and get to work. Right? Unfortunately, getting organized is not quite that easy. Before you start the renovations, you must first look at what you have in the system.

You start by examining your current records system. The examination phase of the process is extremely important. You wouldn't consider walking into your physician's office and declaring "skip the X-rays and blood tests, just give me the treatment." You need to examine the records of those tests before you can determine the "cure."

The examination process identifies the "who, what, where, how, and why" of your records. You will determine:

- Who creates or receives records;
- Who uses the records;
- What records you keep;
- Where you store these records;
- How long you keep the records;
- How you store these records; and
- Why you keep these records.

The examination will take some time, but it is the most important step of the process.

The Records Inventory

The examination begins with a records inventory. A **records inventory** is a detailed listing that could include the types, locations, dates, volumes, equipment, classification systems, and usage data of an organization's records. The records inventory is based on information about your records obtained through a records survey. A **records survey** is a detailed review that gathers basic information about the quantity, type, function, location, and organization of records. A survey of your records is done so that you know exactly what records and information are maintained in your office. The records inventory is the primary tool from which to develop a records management program.

Inventory Preparation

The methods you will use to complete the inventory will depend on the size of your business. The more employees in the business, the more records collected, and the more time needed to complete the inventory.

Where to Begin   Before you start the inventory, collect any existing information you may already have on your records. This information will help in the examination process. Items to collect include:

- Organizational chart
- Filing procedures
- An office layout
- File folder indexes – lists of what is stored in the file cabinets
- File box indexes – lists of the boxes in storage

The size of your organization will determine if you have any of these items. The larger the business, the more likely you are to have some or all these documents. If the business does not have any of these documents, that's okay. Don't create them just for this project.

Where Are the Records?   Take a visual survey of your records storage locations. In each area, begin at the door and sweep from left to right, identifying each storage location.

Identify the conventional storage locations such as file cabinets, desk drawers, shelving units, bookcases, card files, CD stacks, diskette boxes, computer hard drives, hanging map files, etc. Also, note the haphazard file locations such as piles of unfiled records stacked on tops of cabinets, credenzas, desks, and tables, and records piled on the floor. You should also take note of the temporary storage locations, such as to-be-filed baskets and records storage boxes, and the hidden storage areas located in garages, closets, attics, or sheds.

Assign a number to each location. If you have a layout diagram or map of your office, you can create a very helpful visual reference by numbering each storage location directly on the layout. A sample layout with storage locations numbered is shown in Figure 3.1.

Take notes on the character of each storage location. Describe the equipment, noting its size (letter or legal) and the number of shelves or drawers. Also, note the media types within the location. For example, does the equipment contain file folders, binders, diskettes, compact disks, etc? If it contains file folders, describe the type of file folder—letter- or legal-size file folders, top tab or side tab, manila folders, hanging folders, or folders with dividers. Finally, note which employees access the records in this location.

With this information, you will set up a Location Index similar to the one shown in Figure 3.2. This index is the beginning of your inventory plan. It identifies where and how all records are stored, and who accesses these records.

What to Inventory?   Identify all records stored in and around your office area, as well as those you may have stored in hidden areas such as closets, garages, attics, or basements.

Identify the Categories

During the inventory process, you will identify the categories of records your business retains. **File categories**, sometimes referred to as *subjects* or *subject headings*, are collections of related files that are used together and filed together. For example, you will have a collection of files pertaining to accounting functions and another collection relating to purchases. Or, you

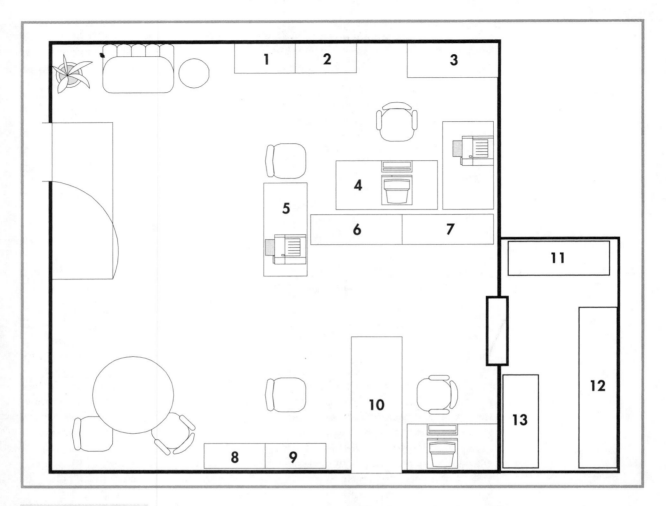

Figure 3.1
Office Layout

might have a personnel file consisting of an application, reference letters, benefit forms, etc. Each collection contains a series of files. Within each file, you will have a collection of related documents. Categories are sometimes referred to as *records series*. A **records series** is a group of related records filed/used together as a unit and evaluated as a unit for retention purposes.

Data collected during this inventory serves as a link to your retention schedule, vital records program, and files management system. Records retention is discussed in detail in Chapter 4. Vital records are discussed in Chapter 5.

Do not confuse file categories with file indexes. The inventory is not a method to identify every file folder, as in an index. The inventory is a method of identifying broad categories represented within the files.

Standard Categories   Records managers are quick to admit that every office filing system is different. As a matter of routine, a records manager prefers to view each office as a unique records environment, with each office possessing its own history, personalities, and procedures.

In reality, most offices maintain a collection of similar records categories that pertain to basic business functions such as accounting, hiring, office management, contract law, and

Data collected during this inventory serves as a link to your retention schedule, vital records program, and files management system.

Figure 3.2

Location Index

Location Index		
Location	Description	Access
1.	bookcase 6 shelves high binders	Martha
2.	vertical file cabinet 5-drawer, letter size hanging folders with manila folder inserts	Martha & Tom
3.	credenza 2 letter-size file drawers plus 2 shelves hanging folders in drawers binders on shelves	Martha
4.	desk drawers 2 drawers, letter size hanging folders	Martha
5.	credenza 2 letter-size file drawers plus 2 shelves hanging folders in drawers supplies on shelves	Tom

property management. How these records categories are organized and accessed may vary from office to office, but they have many similarities.

These records are referred to as *standard categories*. **Standard categories** pertain to office maintenance functions such as personnel, facilities management, administrative (office) functions, and information technology. They are records common to most business offices. We can easily identify these records. See Appendix 1 for a comprehensive listing of standard categories.

Industry-Specific Categories   The remaining records in your office are unique to your business. Dentists maintain patient charts; architects have project files and drawing files; land surveyors use maps and plats; accountants and attorneys maintain client files; and equipment operators manage maintenance and parts records for each piece of equipment. These records are referred to as *industry-specific categories*. **Industry-specific categories** are records maintained that are unique to the industry of the business. These records pertain to the operations and services conducted by the business and to the functions it performs in carrying out the operations and services.

You will identify these records during the course of the inventory. These records are not standard, and your office may maintain some or all these types of records.

Problems During the Inventory

The biggest problem you may typically encounter is that many records are not stored in collections. They are instead arranged in large, alphabetic subject files. Everything is intermixed and difficult to identify. A second problem is that folders are not properly labeled or folder contents are not accurately identified. These problems will slow you down, but you must take time to identify the contents and assign the folder to a category.

- *Mislabels.* Many folders may be unlabeled or mislabeled. As you flip through a folder, you may recognize that the label does not match the contents. Write the correct title on the folder, and if you have an external index for this file, note the correction on the index as well. Mislabeling is an important reason for reviewing folder contents and not taking the folder label as fact.

- *Misfiles.* You may find a file out of sequence. In this instance, replace the file in its proper filing space.

- *Multiple folders for the same information.* In large, alphabetic filing systems, finding two folders for the same subject is not unusual. Materials may have been received at different times, and a new folder was created when the second set of materials was filed. For example, you may have one file labeled "Panasonic Fax Machine" and a second folder, labeled "Fax Machines – Panasonic," filed in another drawer.

- *Outdated materials.* During the course of the inventory, you may come across some out-of-date materials received via mass distribution such as vendor catalogs, promotions on classes, information gathered on equipment, etc. Feel free to toss any outdated materials.

- *Duplicates.* Extra copies of the same document may be tossed, unless you know that copies are being retained for business purposes.

- *Nonrecord supplies.* You may find nonrecord items, such as equipment and supplies, coffee cups, snack food, or party decorations, in your filing cabinets. Remove these items from the file area and store them in areas not reserved for filing.

Conduct the Inventory

Plan to conduct the inventory during a quiet day at the office. If you can, do it on a Saturday, or at least let your answering machine take your calls for a few hours. *Resist the urge to begin sorting and discarding during this process.* You will have plenty of time to do these tasks later. If you so chose, you may keep a trash can close by to toss the obvious discards such as outdated vendor brochures and catalogs, junk mail, notices of past events, etc. <u>Do not</u> discard any legal, financial, or employee information at this time, unless you are certain that it is a duplicate copy.

Ideally, you will do the inventory yourself; but if you must recruit assistance, you may ask your staff or coworkers to inventory their own file areas. If you seek assistance, make certain that the scope and instructions of the inventory are very clear so that the data is uniformly collected.

Inventory Form

Using a form to gather data during the inventory will ensure that you are gathering the information in a consistent and routine manner. The following information should be on the form:

- *Category:* A descriptive title for the file category.

- *Description:* A brief description of the category. The description should include an illustrative list of types of documents routinely filed in this category.

- *Storage methods:* Location of the records and a description of the storage container. If you created a Location Index, as illustrated in Figure 3.2, you may enter the location number where the records are located as a cross-reference to this information.

- *Media:* Identify the records' media. The most commonly used media is paper, but records are frequently maintained in other media such as varied paper media or electronic formats. Some examples of different or varied paper media are oversized maps or drawings, photographs, postcards, business cards, specialized forms, tags, etc. Records stored on nonpaper media may be on magnetic hard drives, magnetic disks, magnetic tape, CD-ROMs, microfilm, CD-RWs, DVDs, videocassettes, X-rays, slides, negatives, etc.

- *File arrangement:* Briefly explain the current filing arrangement and scheme. Identify the arrangement, such as alphabetic, numeric, or chronologic, and then identify the basic filing scheme or element of the arrangement. For example, your note may read: alphabetically by client name; numerically by vendor number; or chronologically by date received.

- *Date range:* Identify the approximate date range of documents in each category.

- *Access:* Identify the frequency with which the records are used. Are they accessed *frequently*, such as daily or weekly? Are they accessed *occasionally*, maybe monthly or quarterly? Or, are they *rarely* accessed, maybe once a year or less? Is the access dependent on age or status of the documents? Do you access the <u>active</u> accounts *frequently*, but the <u>closed</u> accounts *rarely*? Do you access <u>this year's</u> accounts receivables *frequently*, and <u>last year's</u> receivables only *occasionally*?

To expedite the inventory process, an inventory form is available for your use in Appendix 2. You may use it as is, or modify it for your own needs. A portion of a completed inventory worksheet is shown in Figure 3.3.

The standard categories, as defined in Appendix 1, are incorporated into this form. As you inventory your records, you may find other categories. To add an industry-specific category, you can add it to an existing major category, or if suitable, create a new major category.

After the inventory is completed, you will use the data you collected to create the following items:

Figure 3.3

Sample Inventory Worksheet

- Records retention schedule (Chapter 4);

- Vital records program (Chapter 5);

- Filing system (Chapter 6).

ADMINISTRATION Records pertaining to the planning, supervising, and managing of the daily activities of the business.

✔	Category	Container	Media	File Arrangement	Dates	Access
✔	Correspondence/General	Vertical file cabinet – Location 2	Paper	Alphabetic, by name	2002	Frequently
✔	Calendars/Schedules	Vertical file cabinet – Location 2	Paper	By year	2002	Frequently
✔	Meetings/Reports	Lateral file cabinet – Location 1	Paper	By year, by month, alphabetic by name	2001	Occasionally
✔	Memberships	Lateral file cabinet – Location 1 Hard drive – Location 3	Paper; electronic	Alphabetic by name	2002	Occasionally
✔	Equipment/Furniture	Vertical file cabinet – Location 2 Hard drive – Location 3	Paper; electronic	Alphabetic, by vendor	2001 – 2002	Occasionally
✔	Inventory Lists	Hard drive – Location 3	Electronic	Alphabetic, by item	2001 – 2002	Occasionally
✔	Maintenance	Hard drive – Location 3	Electronic	By year, by month	2001 – 2002	Frequently

Chapter 4

What to Keep; When to Toss

For some people, the act of tossing a document is extremely difficult. To the hoarder, the nagging thought in the back of his or her mind is 'The minute I toss this record, I'll need it.' Then, to compound this doubt, sure enough, once or twice in his/her lifetime, he/she will actually toss a document that is needed a few days later. Thus, the hoarding and the paper pileup continue.

If left unchecked, a business can easily double its records storage volume every three to five years.[1] To a one-person company, the need for extra storage may mean buying a new file cabinet or larger disk drives every couple of years. To a larger company, the need for more storage may mean leasing new space as well as buying new file cabinets and more computers every couple of years.

In contrast, some people would rather toss than keep. To an overly organized person, a clean desk is the most important goal. To reach this goal, he/she will sacrifice almost anything to prevent a paper pileup. When he/she believes that the paper or electronic files are out of control, he/she may randomly toss or delete documents to clean up a hard drive or make space in a file cabinet.

This lack of regard for how long records must be kept can be detrimental to a business. Government agencies, such as the Internal Revenue Service or the Occupational Safety & Health Administration, require a business to keep certain records for specified periods of time. Failure to comply can result in severe penalties or fines. In addition, if your business is faced with potential litigation, opposing counsel may call into question your records destruction policy. Can you adequately prove that you did not intentionally destroy the records? If not, sanctions may be imposed. On the other hand, did you destroy records that could corroborate your position? You may lose a legal action because you prematurely destroyed your defending evidence.

To protect the interests of the business, we need to draw on the life cycle of a record. The five stages of a record's life cycle are its creation, distribution, use, maintenance, and retirement, or disposition.[2] All records of a company should cycle through these stages in a routine, predetermined manner.

Records Retention Program

By establishing a records retention program, you will be able to confirm which records are needed to operate the business effectively and the length of time these records must be retained.

The purpose of creating a records retention program is to remove the self-doubt and the second-guessing when deciding what to keep and when to toss. By establishing a records retention program, you will be able to confirm which records are needed to operate the business effectively and the length of time these records must be retained. After the useful life of a record has passed, the record should be destroyed.

Treat Business Records as an Asset

Every business asset has a value attached to it. If an asset were erroneously misplaced, lost, erased, or destroyed, the business would understandably suffer a loss. Although records are not tangible company assets, the content information of some records can be extremely valuable to the business. You should protect and preserve your records as you would any business asset.

Schedule Records in All Formats

The most common records format is paper; however, the records retention schedule that you will prepare based on the records inventory applies to records in all formats. Many records are retained only in electronic form; others may be duplicated in both electronic and paper. *Do not* selectively retain the electronic while destroying the paper, or the reverse.

Remember to create a retention policy and schedule for electronic mail (e-mail). Much business is conducted through e-mail. Consequently, records are being transmitted electronically. You need to decide how to handle e-mail records to assure that records that should be kept *are* kept and that records that should be destroyed *are* destroyed, according to your retention policy and schedule.

Destroy Records on Schedule

Random or selective destruction may create the impression that the records retention program has not been properly implemented and, in the event of pending litigation or government audit, it can be viewed as intentional destruction.

Once a program has been established, records should be routinely destroyed. Destruction should be done in the *ordinary course of business*, meaning that destruction is done as a routine business process. Random or selective destruction may create the impression that the records retention program has not been properly implemented and, in the event of pending litigation or government audit, it can be viewed as *intentional* destruction.

If any hint of litigation or an audit exists, records destruction should be immediately halted. Otherwise, the business could be liable for obstruction of justice or contempt of court charges. As more information becomes available to legal counsel, you may destroy certain records that are outside the scope of the litigation or audit. Once the matter is resolved, or if the threat passes without issue, you may continue your routine destruction processes.

Document Your Retention Research

You should document and substantiate your records retention decisions. If you do your research and document your retention decisions, it will indicate that your business used its "best efforts" to comply with all retention requirements.

Understandably, some legal requirements for records retention can be difficult to determine or interpret. However, a government agency will be less likely to impose fines or penalties on a business if it can demonstrate that it tried to comply with the law. If you have specific issues regarding your retention research, you need to discuss them with your attorney or accountant.

Establish Regular Disposition Routines

Records retention should not be handled piecemeal or randomly. You should establish regular routines as part of your records management program. The routines should be consistent and recurring. For example, you may establish a *Year-end Clean Up Day*. (See Chapter 10.)

Records Appraisal

A records appraisal determines the value of records. A **records appraisal** is the process of evaluating records based on their current operational, regulatory, legal, fiscal, and historical significance, their informational value, arrangement, and their relationship to other records. The value of a record is equal to the need for the record. The greater the need, the higher the value of the record. Similarly, the lower the need, the less likely the business places any value on the record.

Retain Records for a Reason

A business needs to retain records for many reasons. To better understand the need to keep certain records, review the legal and operational needs that a business typically retains records listed in Figure 4.1.

Need for Records

With the inventory of your records in hand (See Chapter 3 for information on how to conduct a records inventory.), the next step is to analyze each record or file category and make decisions about the need for each category. These decisions will be based on the need or value of the records in a category to the business. Apply two needs or values to the business: legal and operational. A records category may have more than one value. For example, benefit plans are maintained to comply with government regulations as well as to meet the operational needs of the records.

- **Legal needs** for records are on based the legal rights or obligations of the records. Records have **legal value** when they provide legal proof of business transactions and/or

Figure 4.1

Reasons for Retaining Records

Legal Needs

1. To document a business transaction.
2. To preserve corporate knowledge and memory.
3. To comply with government regulations.

Operational Needs

4. To manage fiscal assets.
5. To document a financial transaction.
6. To compute and substantiate tax liability.
7. To make decisions about current or future courses of action.
8. To document administrative actions and decisions.
9. To interact with customers and potential customers.
10. To interact with partners, agents, and internal staff.
11. To interact with vendors and sellers.

demonstrate compliance with legal, statutory, and regulatory requirements. Examples of records with legal value are *contracts, titles, leases, legal opinions, financial statements, tax statements, payroll records,* and *licenses.*

Records that document important events of an organization are also those records with legal value applied. These records document and preserve the corporate memory. They include *articles of incorporation, bylaws, resolutions, official meeting minutes,* and *audit records.*

- **Operational needs** apply to those records used in the day-to-day operations of the business. An **operational record** documents those activities of an organization that are directed towards the substantive purpose for which the organization was created. These records may have long-term or short-term needs, and they are retained to track, document, audit, instruct, trace, guide, verify, and explain business practices. Examples include *employee manuals, organizational charts, policy statements, policies and procedures, job descriptions, market research, correspondence, budget documents,* and *vouchers.*

Legal Retention Considerations

In general, records managers do not endorse generic retention schedules. Typically, a records management practitioner would research all federal, state, and local legal regulations for citations that pertain to the type of business in which they are working. The Regulatory Research Report in Appendix 3 summarizes many of the regulations commonly applied to most businesses. (You are strongly advised to review the actual citation, available on the Internet or at your local library, to determine if your business practices are included in the regulation.) The list in Appendix 3 is <u>not</u> all-inclusive; additional research will be necessary.

Although large businesses may have ample resources and personnel for this type of research, small businesses are at a disadvantage. However, the importance of this task cannot be diminished. Resources are available to help you with this research.

Federal Laws

Laws enacted by the United States Congress are translated into rules and regulations and are published by the various agencies that enforce these regulations, within the *Code of Federal Regulations (CFR)* and the *United States Code (USC).*

> Web sites for various federal agencies usually provide a laws and regulations page that identifies the regulations related to that agency.

Web sites for various federal agencies usually provide a laws and regulations page that identifies the regulations related to that agency. A source to begin your research is the official U.S. government Web portal: www.firstgov.gov/.

Hundreds of regulations pertaining to the keeping of records exist. The regulations usually state what records must be kept and, in some, how long they must be kept and/or made available for review, audit, inspection, etc. These regulations may apply to persons or businesses. Some regulations are general and apply to all businesses. Most, however, apply to a specific industry or business that produces a specific type of product or provides a certain type of service.

With so many regulations, how do you know which ones apply to your business? The regulations are arranged by the regulatory agency that oversees the regulation. For example, if your business deals with produce, it is regulated by the Department of Agriculture, CFR Title 7. If pesticides are present, then review the regulations of the Environmental Protection Agency (EPA), CFR Title 40. If employees are exposed to these pesticides, then review the regulations of the Occupational Safety & Health Administration (OSHA), CFR Title 29.

The following government Internet sources can direct you to regulations that apply to your business.

- Department of Agriculture: www.usda.gov/
- Environmental Protection Agency: www.epa.gov/
- Occupational Safety & Health Administration: www.osha.gov/

State Statutes

Researching state statutes is important if your business is regulated at the state level. Examples include insurance, real estate, environmental or biological interactions, hazardous waste, etc. Other businesses that are highly regulated at the state level include banks and savings and loans, but these types of businesses are not usually within the realm of "small business" and therefore are not included in this publication.

Individual state statutes may be reviewed at your library or courthouse, or you can access the statutes from most of the 50 states and the District of Columbia on the Internet. Through the Internet, you can access full-text state statutes. These statutes can usually be accessed by logging on to the government Web page for your state and looking for links to legislation or statutes (referred to as codes or compiled laws in some states).

Search hints: Most sites have keyword searches. Because you may not know the exact statute phrasing, some keywords to search include *records, retain, retention,* or *keep.*

Limitations of Actions

Of particular importance to records retention research are the limitations of action or statutes of limitation. A **statute of limitations** is a period of time in which legal action can be taken. Federal, state, and provincial statutes of limitation should be considered when developing retention periods of records. Appendix 4 contains a brief overview of state statutes of limitations for written documents, property damage, and personal injury.

Statutes of limitation are the rules of law governing the period of time during which a claim must be filed. These statutes are laws, passed by legislation, recorded in the state statutes for each state, and vary by state. Statues of limitations are not requirements to keep records, and you do not have to retain records throughout the entire statute of limitations period. These statutes are just guides to be used to weigh the benefits or risks of retaining your records.

Many attorneys may advise you to keep your records for the full statute of limitations period so that, in case of litigation, the records are available. This recommendation is based on two assumptions: (1) that litigation will occur, and (2) that the records will be more helpful than harmful. Whether to retain records throughout the full statutory period or not requires some thinking. A delicate balance exists between the costs associated with retaining versus the risks associated with tossing. A good rule of thumb is that if your company has a history of litigation, keeping the records the full period may be a worthwhile, conservative measure. If your company has little or no history of litigation, then proceeding with a shorter retention period is the better alternative, with the understanding that if litigation appears foreseeable or eminent, all records destruction will cease.

Additional Resources

Additional sources for retention research are available. For example:

- Some professional organizations and associations have researched the regulations and set up industry-specific retention schedules that are available to their members.

- Many law firms and CPA firms have prepared retention schedules that they have made available to their clients. Use these schedules with caution, however, if the schedule was not researched or created by the firm that supplied it to you. Generic, mass-produced retention schedules are not good records retention sources.

- You may choose to hire a records management consultant to research the statutes for you.

- ARMA International also has available other resources such as how-to guidebooks on retention research, as well as access to software containing databases of many of the records retention citations, sorted by industry type. Various ARMA International resources are listed in Appendix 6. All ARMA International resources are available at www.arma.org.

Regulatory Research Report

All your research findings should be documented in a regulatory research report. This report will explain your regulatory references and support your records retention decisions. Appendix 3 contains a model of a regulatory research report containing research for common business records. An excerpt from that model report is shown in Figure 4.3.

The information most commonly contained in this report includes the following:

- *Code:* A unique abbreviated identifier for each regulation.

- *Citation:* The specific federal and/or state code that stipulates the retention period. A full federal regulation citation, which consists of the title+ CFR+ section number. Once a regulation is completed and has been printed in the Federal Register as a final rule, it is "codified" by being published in the Code of Federal Regulations (CFR). The CFR is the official record of all regulations created by the United States federal government. It is divided into 50 volumes, called *titles*, each of which focuses on a particular area. For example, most tax regulations appear in Title 26.

- *Agency:* The agency that issued the regulation and that will enforce it.

- *Records Summary:* A short description of the types of records referenced in the regulation.

Figure 4.3

Sample Regulatory Research Report

Regulatory Research Report				
Code	Citation	Agency	Records Summary	Retention Period
Accounting, Finance, and Tax				
AFT-01	26 CFR 1.57-5(a)	Internal Revenue Service, Department of the Treasury	Records of amounts expended and adjustments made to property acquired and held for investment or to verify excessive use of qualified stock option plan.	Indefinite
AFT-02	26 CFR 1.57-5(b)	Internal Revenue Service, Department of the Treasury	Net operating losses.	Indefinite
AFT-03	26 CFR 1.162-17	Internal Revenue Service, Department of the Treasury	Records to substantiate ordinary and necessary business expenses of travel, transportation, and entertainment concerning the performance of services as an employee.	Not specified

● *Retention Period:* The length of time a record is to be retained, according to the regulation. If a regulation cites that records should be retained but a term of retention was not identified, enter "Not Specified" into this field.

Developing a Records Retention Schedule

Like any schedule, the retention schedule is a timetable that indicates what records to keep and when to destroy records.

You are now ready to develop a records retention schedule. A **records retention schedule** is a comprehensive list of records categories or records series titles, indicating for each series the length of time it is to be maintained. The schedule may include retention in active office areas, inactive storage areas, and when and if such series may be destroyed or formally transferred to another entity such as an archives for historical preservation. Like any schedule, the retention schedule is a timetable that indicates what records to keep and when to destroy records.

A model retention schedule is included in Appendix 5. The schedule is a compilation of retention guidelines for common business records.

To build a customized records retention schedule, start with a table similar to the one below.

1. **Category:** List all records categories (records series) that you found in your inventory.

	Category
ACC	ACCOUNTING
ACC-01	ACCOUNTS PAYABLE
ACC-01-01	Invoices
ACC-01-02	Expense Accounts
ACC-01-03	Contributions
ACC-01-04	Ledger
ACC-01-05	Reports

2. **Regulatory Research:** Where applicable, apply the relevant regulatory research on retention to the category.

	Category	Regulatory Research	
ACC	ACCOUNTING	Codes	Retention Period
ACC-01	ACCOUNTS PAYABLE		
ACC-01-01	Invoices	AFT-08	Not specified
		AFT-12, AFT-13	3Y
ACC-01-02	Expense Accounts	AFT-03 or AFT-05	Not specified
ACC-01-03	Contributions	AFT-04, AFT-06	Not Specified
		AFT-13	3Y
ACC-01-04	Ledger	AFT-08	Indefinite
ACC-01-05	Reports		

Not all records categories will have applicable regulatory citations. Leave this section blank if no legal citation exists.

	Category	Regulatory Research	
ADM	ADMINISTRATION	Codes	Retention Period
ADM-01	CORRESPONDENCE / GENERAL		
ADM-02	CALENDARS / SCHEDULES		
ADM-03	MEETINGS / REPORTS		
ADM-04	MEMBERSHIPS		

3. **Retention Period:** Finally, enter the total retention for each records series or category of records. You may use the periods shown in the Model Retention Schedule in Appendix 5 as a reference. The guidelines in the schedule suggest <u>minimum</u> retention periods for the records categories listed. Where applicable, <u>minimum</u> retention periods required by regulatory authorities are identified.

Quick Tip for Your Legal or Tax Advisor: Three-Year Retention Presumption

Citing the Federal Paperwork Reduction Act of 1980 and the Uniform Preservation of Private Business Records Act, one records retention authority argues that a "presumption" may be applied if no term is stated; businesses should retain records for three years, but they have no duty to keep them thereafter.[3] The Uniform law or its equivalent has been adopted (at the time of this writing) by Colorado, Georgia, Illinois, Maryland, New Hampshire, North Dakota, Oklahoma, and Texas. This presumption should at best be viewed as a rule of thumb for guidance in setting a records retention policy.

To customize the schedule, you must take into consideration the legal retention as well as your operational needs for each category of records. To determine your operational needs, estimate how long the records are needed in the day-to-day operations of your business. Review the schedule guidelines and adjust the time as necessary.

Retention periods are expressed in the Model Retention Schedule in Appendix 5 as a code. The following codes are used:

- ACT (Active): Keep while active and until matter is terminated, closed, or completed, e.g., while the contract is in effect, the insurance policy is in force, you own the property, the license is valid, etc.
- AR (Annual Review): Review periodically to determine if material is still current and up-to-date.
- ATA (After Tax or Audit): Keep until tax filing date or final audit is completed.
- C (Creation): Point of creation.
- CY (Current Year): Current calendar or fiscal year.
- Y (Years): Number of years.
- IND (Indefinite): Keep for an open-ended time period.
- SUP (Superseded): Keep until obsolete and/or replaced.
- + (Plus): Add the components, e.g., CY+4Y = Current year plus four years, C+1Y = Point of creation plus one year.

● SC (State Considerations): Considerations of state statutes that may influence retention requirements.

The codes are then connected to create a retention formula: **starting point + number**. A starting point indicates the point at which the retention period begins, such as from creation, until no longer active, or after audit; the number identifies the number of years to retain. For example:

● CY+5Y reads as current year plus five years. If the record was created in 2001, then it is retained for the rest of 2001, plus 2002, 2003, 2004, 2005, 2006, and can be destroyed in January 2007.

● ACT+6Y reads as from end of active period (e.g., termination of contract, end of employment, no longer a client) plus three years. If the contract was in effect from March 2001 through March 2003, the contract is retained through March 2003, plus 2004, 2005, 2006, 2007, 2008, and eligible for destruction in March 2009.

	Category	Regulatory Research		Retention Period
		Codes	Retention Period	
ADM	ACCOUNTING			Keep
ACC-01	ACCOUNTS PAYABLE			CY+5Y
ACC-01-01	Invoices	AFT-08	Not specified	CY+5Y
		AFT-12	3Y	
		AFT-13	3Y	
ACC-01-02	Expense Accounts	AFT-03 or AFT-05	Not specified	CY+5Y
ACC-01-03	Contributions	AFT-04, AFT-06	Not Specified	CY+5Y
		AFT-13	3Y	
ACC-01-04	Ledger	AFT-08	Indefinite	CY+5Y
ACC-01-05	Reports			CY+5Y

Notes

1. David O. Stephens, "Megatrends in Records Management," *Records Management Quarterly* 27, no. 1 (January 1993): 38.

2. Judy Read-Smith, Mary L. Ginn, and Norman F. Kallaus, *Records Management*, 7th ed. (Cincinnati, OH: South-Western / Thomson Publishing Co., 2002), 14.

3. Donald J. Skupsky, J.D., CRM, Editor, *Legal Requirements for Business Records: Federal Requirements* (Denver: Information Requirements Clearinghouse, 1998).

Quick Tip for Your Legal or Tax Advisor: Seven-Year Retention Myth

You may have heard of a common misconception in the business world that records should be kept for a minimum of seven years. This seven-year edict does not exist in the real world. The appraisal and research process will reveal numerous ways to schedule records and that "one size" does not fit all.

Chapter 5

Disasters ...
Yes, They Can Happen to You

"**I** can't think about that right now." "It won't happen here." "I have other, more important things to worry about." What information do you need before you realize that a few extra, protective steps can protect your investments from "going up in flames?"

Small business owners are particularly vulnerable to disasters. In the early days of a new enterprise, a successful day is just scraping by, and building the business is the primary task. When the business takes off, you are too busy with day-to-day maintenance of the business to think about disasters. Don't wait for a hard drive failure or a fire to make a believer out of you. You just may be too late to take steps to protect your business.

Vital Records

Vital records are those records within the business that are essential to the continuation of your business if a disaster strikes. Such records are necessary to re-create the organization's legal and financial status and to determine the rights and obligations of employees, customers, stockholders (if any), and citizens. The loss or destruction of these records would seriously impede the continuation of the business. Placing a value on business records is not an easy task. You may be tempted to save every piece of paper. In reality, very few records are truly vital to an organization. Records management experts estimate that less than 5 percent of your records are classified as vital records.

> The loss or destruction of these records would seriously impede the continuation of the business.

When evaluating your records, review your critical business functions. The records that support these functions are used to establish the legal and financial positions of your business. They are used also to meet your legal and financial obligations to your customers, employees, and shareholders. A sample list of vital records is provided in Figure 5.1.

Other records that should be protected are the *unique / irreplaceable records*, such as one-of-a-kind maps, drawings, graphics, formulas, recipes, and *historical / sentimental records* such as photographs, awards, and ceremonial documents.

Disasters

When we hear the word *disaster*, we normally think of the major disasters we read about in newspapers such as earthquakes, hurricanes, floods, fires, tornadoes, and terrorist attacks. Just as devastating, but with greater likelihood, are the small, localized disasters such as the following:

Figure 5.1

Sample List of Vital Records

Vital Records

Accounting / Finance / Fixed Assets
- Accounts receivable / customer billings
- Bank account information
- General ledgers, journal entries
- Insurance policies
- Lines of credit
- Payroll register

Clients / Customers
- Customer contact information

Corporate / Legal
- Active agreements, contracts, leases
- Active deeds, mortgages
- Board minutes
- Bylaws
- Stockholder registers

Marketing / Sales
- Mailing lists
- Price lists
- Supplier or vendor lists

Personnel
- Benefit plans
- Medical histories
- Employee home telephone numbers

Production
- Inventory
- Patents, formulas
- Quality control
- Technical specifications

- Computer viruses, hardware failures, disk drive crashes
- Human error, human sabotage
- Theft, vandalism, riots
- Leaky or broken water pipes
- Toxic mold
- Power fluctuations, including power outages, power spikes, and brownouts
- Insect and rodent infestation
- Coffee, soft drinks, or food spilling onto documents or into computers

> The scope of a vital records program depends on the extent of a potential disaster.

Take a moment to evaluate the risks. What kinds of disasters could hit your business? The scope of a vital records program depends on the extent of a potential disaster. From what are you protecting your records? Do you live in "tornado alley"? Are you in a potential hurricane path? Are you located in a high-crime area? Do you have any potentially volatile employees? Are you located along a very busy street or highway? Are hazardous materials or potentially hazardous types of facilities, such as gas stations or propane tanks, positioned nearby? Do tanker trucks or trains full of hazardous and/or combustible materials pass your location? Do you store records in potentially unstable locations such as in basements, storage sheds, or miniwarehouses?

Disasters regularly strike our communities. At minimum, they are minor disruptions; at worst, the business is destroyed. According to the National Fire Protection Association (NFPA), of the businesses that suffer major fire damage, as many as 65 percent fail to reopen.[1]

The following examples illustrate just how quickly a disaster can occur.

Diane runs a professional catering business out of her home kitchen. She has an impressive recipe collection that she keeps on an old desktop computer in her kitchen. She periodically updates the recipes, making adjustments or adding new recipes. She also maintains a detailed client list on the computer. She considers the contents of both databases to be her "trade secrets." Diane is very careful to protect her secrets—she does not keep any printed lists or extra copies available, nor does she allow access to either database without a password.

One morning while logging onto the computer, it made a horrible screeching sound. She quickly called a computer-savvy friend, who upon assessing the problem, declared that the hard drive had crashed and that he could do nothing about it. Without a paper or electronic backup available, Diane lost everything.

Ernie runs a small mail-order business in the warehouse area of the city. His computer network is a new, state-of-the-art system. He is very meticulous in his instructions to his staff that a backup of the daily accounting and inventory system be made nightly. His old system had been a nightmare to maintain, and he is not yet comfortable with the new system. He is determined not to lose this data. Nightly, his staff creates a backup of the data and transfers the data to tapes, which they store in a supply cabinet adjacent to the server.

One night, around midnight, Ernie received a call from his security company informing him that the burglar alarm had just gone off. The office area of his warehouse had likely been broken into. He kept no cash on-site, so he couldn't think of what the burglars would want. Upon arriving at the office, he found all the brand-new high-tech equipment gone... including all the back-up tapes.

Protection Methods

Several protection methods can be put into practice to protect your vital records. These methods include making duplicates of records and storing them in off-site locations, using fire-resistant cabinets, and using various data-protection methods.

Duplication and Dispersal

Routinely create extra copies and store these copies off-site. You can easily make extra copies by:

- Photocopying
- Imaging the documents onto a CD-ROM or optical disk
- Backing up the data onto a removable media such as floppy disks, magnetic tapes, CD-ROMs, or digital audio tapes (DAT) tapes
- Vaulting the data electronically onto a remote computer via the Internet or a modem

Distribute these extra copies to a location that is *separate and away from your primary place of business.* If you are concerned about a major environmental disaster, then the second location should be at least 50 miles from the primary location. Good locations to use are branch offices, commercial records centers, or safe-deposit boxes. If you have a home office, you could arrange with another home-based business to exchange vital records storage areas.

Fire-Resistant Equipment

The use of insulated fire-resistant file cabinets or vaults may be a practical protection method for small businesses. Most of these cabinets are designed to protect paper under severe temperature conditions. If you store other media, such as magnetic tapes or disks, be sure to check the manufacturers' specifications to ensure that the equipment will adequately protect the media in a fire.

Although using fire-resistant cabinets may be an easy protection method to implement, it is not always the best. The use of this method is based on the assumption that you can get access to the file cabinet or vault after a disaster. In some instances, such as after an earthquake or explosion, the building may not be stable enough to allow entrance.

Data Protection Methods

Protecting electronic data from intentional or accidental corruption should be addressed as well. The following methods are recommended for protecting electronic data.

- Conduct routine maintenance of your operating system, as recommended by the system, to ensure optimum operation.
- Employ routine (preferably daily, at minimum weekly) back-up processes. Remove the back-up media from the computer system and store it in a secure place, preferably a remote location.
- Keep a "build book" in which to note when software was added to your system. In the event of a system failure, the build book can be used by a technician to determine if incompatible software is at fault.
- Install a high-quality surge protector for all computer equipment.
- Establish a password protection routine for data protection.
- Install virus checking and firewall software.
- Do not open any e-mail attachments from unknown sources.

If data is lost, a company that specializes in data recovery may be able to recover most or all of it. These data recovery companies use sophisticated equipment to recover information from hard drives damaged by mechanical malfunctions, fire, water, etc. The recovery process is expensive, however. Moreover, it may take several weeks to complete, and a data recovery company usually offers no guarantees that all or any of the data can be recovered.

Vital Records Protection / Business Continuity Plan

If the building in which your business is located were destroyed or became unstable, a vital records protection or business continuity plan lays in place the actions necessary to get the business back into business. Which records would you need to reconstruct the company? Whom would you need to contact?

Remember all the fire drills you had to go through in elementary and high school? They were necessary for students, teachers, and other school employees to know what to do if a fire started. The same precautions apply in business as well. You need to have a plan and practice it so that you know what to do if an emergency occurs.

Begin by establishing a recovery team and designating a team leader who is the final decision-maker and primary spokesperson. Sole proprietors may want to include family members on this team. The following items need to be prepared as part of your plan. All team members need to have the latest copies of any and all lists and other plan information.

1. Keep a telephone listing of all team members arranged in call-priority order. Make certain every team member has a current copy of the list.

2. Keep a list of companies that specialize in emergency situations such as plumbers, electricians, maintenance and repair services, pest control services, janitorial services, rental equipment, fire and water damage restoration, etc. Make certain every team member has a current copy.

If the building in which your business is located were destroyed or became unstable, a vital records protection or business continuity plan lays in place the actions necessary to get the business back into business.

3. Keep a list of companies that specialize in data recovery from hard drives damaged by mechanical malfunctions, fire, water, etc. Make certain every team member has a current copy.

4. Keep a list of companies that specialize in salvage and recovery of paper from fire and water damage. Make certain every team member has a current copy.

5. Establish a procedure to move the business to a remote site if the primary place of business is unstable or inaccessible.

6. Make periodic checks of the validity of your computer backups to assure that your data can be restored from the back-up media.

7. Prepare a Vital Records Master List. A Vital Records Master List provides critical information to the recovery team because it identifies which records are protected and where the records are located. This list should be kept current and in a safe but accessible location. Make certain every team member has a current copy.

   A sample Vital Records Master list is shown in Figure 5.2. The following items should be included on this master list:

   ● *ID:* Assign a unique ID number to each vital record.
   ● *Category Code:* Identify the category code of the vital record.
   ● *Description:* List the document name or give a brief description of the records.
   ● *Dept.:* If applicable, identify the department that is responsible for the records.
   ● *Frequency:* Identify when records are transferred to a vital records protection location.
   ● *Retention:* Identify how long records are retained at the vital records protection location.
   ● *Media:* Identify the media of the stored records. If applicable, identify the program or software.
   ● *Location:* Identify where the records are stored.

8. Practice periodically. Rehearse your reaction to certain disasters to determine if your recovery procedures work.

Figure 5.2

Vital Records Master List

Vital Records Master List – January 2002							
ID	Category Code	Description	Dept.	Frequency	Retention	Media	Location
01	ACC-02-01	Accounts Payable	Accounting	Daily/ Incremental	2 weeks	Mag Tape Peachtree	Media Vault
02	ACC-02-01	Accounts Payable	Accounting	Weekly/ Full	4 weeks	Mag Tape Peachtree	Grove Street Warehouse
12	COR-02-01	Board Minutes	Executive	Monthly	Permanent	Paper	Grove Street Warehouse
21	FIN-07	Insurance Policies	Executive	As needed	Replaced	Paper	Grove Street Warehouse
27	HR-07	Personnel Contact Lists	HR	As needed	Replaced	Paper	Grove Street Warehouse

Be Prepared

Know where the vital records are stored and whom to call for help.

Telling yourself that a disaster can't happen in your business will serve no useful purpose. Current events have proven otherwise. You need to be prepared. Know exactly what your business needs to do in a time of crisis. Know where the vital records are stored and whom to call for help. The welfare of your business may depend upon these preparations.

Here are some questions you need to be asking yourself and your staff. You should know the answers to these questions before a disaster happens.

1. Do you have a complete and accurate listing of all employees and their emergency contact information? Do you have employees' cell-phone numbers on this list? Where is this list located?

2. In the event of a disaster, who will verify that all staff are accounted for? Who will contact victims' families?

3. In the event of a disaster, who should be notified of a work slowdown or stoppage? Clients? Colleagues? Suppliers? Dealers? Contractors? Do you have this contact information? Where is it located?

4. If the office or facility is uninhabitable, where will you relocate? Who has the authority to set up this site? What supplies, equipment, and software are needed at this site? What records will you need and where are these backups located?

5. If the office or facility became unstable, e.g., from an earthquake or explosion, but you were allowed back into the area for a ten-minute retrieval and recovery period, what would you retrieve? Do you know exactly where these items are located?

6. Who will manage the recovery project? What outside companies or specialists are available? Do you have a list of this contact information? Where is this list located?

7. Do you have insurance information available? Do you have photographs or other identifying information, such as model numbers and year purchased, of your insured assets? If so, where are they stored?

8. Do you have bank account and loan information available? Where is this information?

9. What legal concerns could arise? Do you have succession instructions? Where is this information? Would a power of attorney be necessary? If so, who can arrange for it?

10. If the office or facility is compromised, what security measures are necessary to protect the remaining assets? Who can provide this security?

Notes

1. Nancy Opiela, "When Misfortune Brings a Client to Your Door," *Journal of Financial Planners* 14, no. 2 (February 2001): 58.

Chapter 6

File Records So That You Can Find Them

L et's review what we've learned so far:

- **Inventory:** We know what records we have.
- **Retention:** We know what records we must keep.
- **Vital Records:** We know what records we must protect.

Now we need to know whether we can find the records. To find records, we must have a filing system. Without a filing system, finding anything is difficult. As the number of documents increases, locating a desired record becomes more difficult, if not impossible.

Establish a Filing System

The goal of every filing system is to provide quick and accurate access to information; in other words, to find records and information. Higher productivity with lower costs is the main benefit of a good filing system. The right system will produce the following results:

- Faster filing and retrieval of records
- Fewer misfiles
- Less time spent filing records
- Less office space needed for filing equipment
- Fewer lost documents, resulting in improved response to litigation discovery and governmental audits

> Higher productivity with lower costs is the main benefit of a good filing system.

File Categories

Standard file categories were introduced in Chapter 3. File categories are the backbone of your filing system, and they are the basis for grouping and organizing your files.

Many offices have informal lists of the types of records they maintain. Usually these lists consist of very broad, generic topics such as accounting, clients, marketing, research, etc.; and some offices may loosely group their records according to these topics.

To be successful, however, a filing system needs consistency, form, and structure. The standard file categories document the form and structure of your filing system. Every document in your office is assigned to a category and filed by that category.

File Codes

File codes are assigned to each category. The codes provide an abbreviated symbol of the category title. Codes are much more efficient than writing out the entire category title. File codes aid filing by:

- *Sorting.* Write the file codes on the documents to be filed. Documents are then presorted into code order before filing.
- *Filing.* Codes are much easier to match than an entire title caption. While filing, match the file code on a document to the file code on a folder.

Subject file codes, shown in Figure 6.1, are broken into three parts: (1) the letters, which identify the subject of the major category; (2) the first two numbers, which identify the primary category; and (3) the last two numbers, which identify the secondary category. A complete listing of the file codes is shown in Table 6.1.

Creating a File Plan

During the course of your inventory, you identified the categories that exist in your office. In preparation for creating your own customized file plan, now is the time to reduce categories from the standard category listing to a representative list of the types of records filed in your office. Begin by reviewing the Standard Category list in Appendix 1 and crossing off the list those categories that are not represented in your filing system (see Figure 6.2).

If, in the course of the inventory, you identified records that were not included in the standard category list, you may customize the categories by adding your industry-specific needs. You will review the principles of creating and adding new subject categories in the following section.

Future Plans

If you are just setting up your business, you most likely have very few, if any records in the inventory. Nevertheless, you should be able to anticipate the categories of records you will be collecting in the future. A similar situation may apply for an established but expanding business as well. While you are setting up your file plan, include those file categories that you foresee using

Figure 6.1

Category Levels of Subject File Codes

MAJOR

ACC ACCOUNTING

Primary

ACC-01 ACCOUNTS PAYABLE

Secondary

ACC-01-01 Invoices   ACC-01-02 Expense Accounts

Primary

ACC-02 ACCOUNTS RECEIVABLE

Secondary

ACC-02-01 Billing / Invoices   ACC-02-02 Reports   ACC-02-03 Collections

Table 6.1

Sample Standard Category Codes

Code	Name
ACC	ACCOUNTING
ACC-01	ACCOUNTS PAYABLE
ACC-01-01	Invoices
ACC-01-02	Expense Accounts
ACC-01-03	Ledger / Register
ACC-01-04	Reports
ACC-02	ACCOUNTS RECEIVABLE
ACC-02-01	Billing / Invoices
ACC-02-02	Reports
ACC-02-03	Collections
ACC-03	CASH MANAGEMENT
ACC-03-01	Journal
ACC-04	COST ACCOUNTING
ACC-04-01	Cost Ledger
ACC-05	GENERAL LEDGER
ACC-05-01	Journal
ACC-05-02	Subledgers
ACC-05-03	Supporting Documents
ACC-06	PAYROLL
ACC-06-01	Payroll / Registers
ACC-06-02	Time Sheets
ACC-06-03	Reports
ACC-06-04	W-2 Forms
ACC-06-05	W-4 Forms
ACC-07	TAX COMPLIANCE
ACC-07-01	Income Tax Returns
ACC-07-02	Payroll / Employment Tax Returns
ACC-07-03	Property Tax Returns
ACC-07-04	Sales Tax Returns
ACC-07-05	Self-Employment Tax Returns
ADM	ADMINISTRATION
ADM-01	CORRESPONDENCE / GENERAL
ADM-02	CALENDARS / SCHEDULES
ADM-03	MEETINGS / REPORTS
ADM-04	MEMBERSHIPS
ADM-05	EQUIPMENT / FURNITURE
ADM-05-01	Inventory Lists
ADM-05-02	Maintenance
ADM-05-03	Manuals
ADM-05-04	Warranties
ADM-06	FACILITIES
ADM-06-01	Building Maintenance
ADM-06-02	Security
ADM-06-03	Space Planning / Plans
ADM-07	FORMS / SUPPLIES
ADM-08	POLICY AND PROCEDURES
ADM-09	RECORDS MANAGEMENT
ADM-09-01	Manuals

Code	Name
ADM-09-02	Retention Schedule
ADM-10	VENDORS
ADM-11	CONSULTANTS
ADM-12	CONTRACTORS / SUBCONTRACTORS
ADM-13	OFFICE FUNCTIONS
ADM-14	PRESENTATION MATERIALS
ADM-15	REFERENCE
CR	CLIENT RELATIONS
CR-01	CLIENTS / ACCOUNTS
CR-02	PROJECTS / SPECIAL PROJECTS
CR-03	COMPLAINTS
COR	CORPORATE
COR-01	ARTICLES OF INCORPORATION/ BYLAWS
COR-02	BOARD OF DIRECTORS
COR-02-01	Minutes / Meetings
COR-02-02	Committees / Meetings
COR-03	SHAREHOLDERS
COR-03-01	Annual Reports
COR-03-02	SEC Reports
COR-04	STOCKS
COR-04-01	Dividend Records
FIN	FINANCE
FIN-01	ASSETS
FIN-01-01	Fixed Assets
FIN-01-02	Depreciation
FIN-01-03	Inventory
FIN-02	AUDITS
FIN-02-01	Internal
FIN-02-02	External
FIN-03	BANKING
FIN-03-01	Statements
FIN-03-02	Canceled Checks
FIN-03-03	Foreign Accounts
FIN-03-04	Petty Cash Fund
FIN-03-05	Reconciliations
FIN-04	BUDGETS
FIN-05	BUSINESS / FINANCIAL PLANS
FIN-06	CONTRIBUTIONS
FIN-07	FINANCIAL SERVICES
FIN-08	FINANCIAL STATEMENTS
FIN-09	INSURANCE POLICIES
FIN-10	INVESTMENTS
FIN-11	LOANS / CREDIT
FIN-12	PURCHASING
FIN-12-01	Purchase Orders
FIN-12-02	Vendor Information

Table 6.1 (continued)

Sample Standard Category Codes

Code	Name	Code	Name
HR	**HUMAN RESOURCES**	LEG-07-01	Deeds / Titles
HR-01	BENEFIT / PENSION PLANS	LEG-07-02	Easements / Right of Ways
HR-01-01	Medical Plans	LEG-07-03	Leases
HR-01-02	Pension Plans	**MS**	**MARKETING & SALES**
HR-01-03	Workers' Compensation	MS-01	ADVERTISING
HR-02	COMPENSATION	MS-02	CONTACT MANAGEMENT
HR-02-01	Compensation Plans	MS-03	DISTRIBUTORS
HR-02-02	Job Descriptions	MS-04	EVENTS
HR-03	HANDBOOK / MANUALS	MS-05	MARKET RESEARCH
HR-04	RECRUITMENT / STAFFING	MS-06	MARKET PLAN
HR-04-01	Applications / Resumes	MS-07	INDUSTRY COMPETITION
HR-04-02	Temporary / Seasonal	MS-07-01	Press Clippings / Trade Articles
HR-05	INS I-9 FORMS		
HR-06	ORGANIZATION CHARTS	MS-08	PUBLIC RELATIONS / PUBLICITY
HR-07	PERSONNEL	MS-08-01	Newsletters
HR-07-01	Employee Files	MS-08-02	Press Releases
HR-07-02	Employee Confidential Files	MS-09	SALES
HR-07-02	Reports	MS-09-01	Bids / Proposals
HR-08	EMPLOYEE DEVELOPMENT	MS-09-02	Orders
HR-09	SAFETY / HEALTH	MS-09-03	Price Lists
HR-09-01	Compliance	MS-09-04	Promotions
HR-09-02	Inspections	MS-09-05	Reports
HR-09-03	Employee Confidential Medical Files	**OP**	**OPERATIONS**
HR-09-04	Employee Confidential Medical Files / Exposure	OP-01	ENVIRONMENTAL HEALTH
		OP-01-01	Reports / Allegations
HR-09-05	Training	OP-02	PRODUCTS
HR-10	LABOR RELATIONS	OP-02-01	Reports / Status
IT	**INFORMATION TECHNOLOGY**	OP-02-02	Work Orders
IT-01	SYSTEMS / DOCUMENTATION	OP-03	SERVICE / WARRANTY
IT-01-01	Hardware	OP-03-01	Claims / Requests
IT-01-02	ISP	OP-03-02	Reports
IT-01-03	Network	OP-04	INSTALLATION / TRANSPORTATION / SHIPPING
IT-01-04	Software		
IT-01-05	Telecommunications	OP-04-01	Bills of Lading
IT-02	WEB DEVELOPMENT / E-COMMERCE	OP-04-02	Exports
		OP-04-03	Packing Lists
IT-03	TRAINING	OP-04-04	Shipping
LEG	**LEGAL**	OP-05	QUALITY
LEG-01	CONTRACTS / AGREEMENTS	OP-05-01	Quality Control
LEG-01-01	General	**RR**	**REFERENCE / RESEARCH**
LEG-01-02	Warranty	RR-01	REFERENCE
LEG-02	CORRESPONDENCE - LEGAL	RR-01-01	Industry
LEG-03	INTELLECTUAL PROPERTY	RR-01-02	Management
LEG-04	LITIGATION / CLAIMS	RR-01-03	IT
LEG-05	OUTSIDE COUNSEL	RR-02	RESEARCH & DEVELOPMENT
LEG-06	PERMITS / LICENSES	RR-02-01	Product development
LEG-07	REAL PROPERTY	RR-02-02	Technical Papers / References
		RR-03	STANDARDS

Figure 6.2

**Editing Standard
Categories**

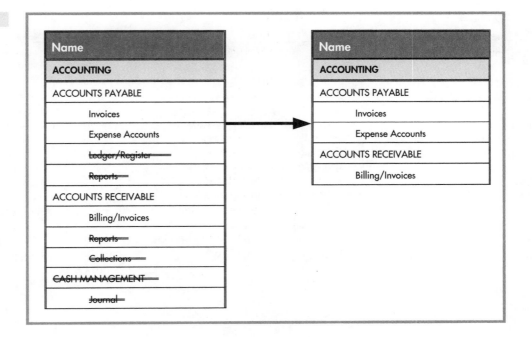

as your business grows. For example, you may not currently have any employees, but as your business expands, you may anticipate hiring. In this case, you may want to incorporate categories pertaining to payroll and human resources into your file plan now.

Code Renumbering

Once you have all categories identified, you may consider renumbering the coding scheme. For example, the sample file plan in Table 6.2, was developed for a small service-type business without any employees. If the developer of the file plan does not anticipate the business using the eliminated categories, he or she may renumber the subcategories into consecutive numeric order. However, once a file code has been assigned and records filed with this code, the code cannot be changed or reused. Any categories added later must be tacked onto the end of the list.

Customize the Standard Categories

The standard categories are comprised of the typical subjects found in most offices. These categories, however, may not exactly fit your business. The standard categories may not include the *industry-specific records* that you maintain. The good news is that you can customize these categories to fit your business.

Design applications and principles to help you develop a subject filing system are presented next. They are the same guidelines that filing system analysts may use. They will help you reach the right decisions when developing a system that suits the needs of your business.

Hierarchy of Subjects

The categories are organized into a hierarchical subject-based outline. They are arranged into major categories, further defined into primary categories, and if necessary, into secondary categories.

Table 6.2

Sample File Plan

Code	Name	Code	Name
ACC	ACCOUNTING	FIN-05	BUSINESS / FINANCAL PLANS
ACC-01	ACCOUNTS PAYABLE	FIN-06	CONTRIBUTIONS
ACC-01-01	Invoices	FIN-07	FINANCIAL SERVICES
ACC-01-02	Expense Accounts	FIN-08	FINANCIAL STATEMENTS
ACC-02	ACCOUNTS RECEIVABLE	FIN-09	INSURANCE POLICIES
ACC-02-01	Billing / Invoices	FIN-10	INVESTMENTS
ACC-05	GENERAL LEDGER	FIN-11	LOANS / CREDIT
ACC-05-01	Journal	FIN-12	PURCHASING
ACC-05-03	Supporting Documents	FIN-12-02	Vendor Information
ACC-07	TAX COMPLIANCE	IT	INFORMATION TECHNOLOGY
ACC-07-01	Income Tax Returns	IT-01	SYSTEMS / DOCUMENTATION
ACC-07-03	Property Tax Returns	IT-01-01	Hardware
ACC-07-04	Sales Tax Returns	IT-01-02	ISP
ACC-07-05	Self-Employment Tax Returns	IT-01-03	Network
ADM	ADMINISTRATION	IT-01-04	Software
ADM-01	CORRESPONDENCE / GENERAL	IT-01-05	Telecommunications
ADM-02	CALENDARS / SCHEDULES	IT-02	WEB DEVELOPMENT / E-COMMERCE
ADM-04	MEMBERSHIPS	IT-03	TRAINING
ADM-05	EQUIPMENT / FURNITURE	LEG	LEGAL
ADM-05-01	Inventory Lists	LEG-01	CONTRACTS / AGREEMENTS
ADM-05-02	Maintenance	LEG-01-01	General
ADM-05-03	Manuals	LEG-01-02	Warranty
ADM-05-04	Warranties	LEG-02	CORRESPONDENCE - LEGAL
ADM-06	FACILITIES	LEG-06	PERMITS / LICENSES
ADM-06-01	Building Maintenance	LEG-07	REAL PROPERTY
ADM-07	FORMS / SUPPLIES	LEG-07-01	Deeds / Titles
ADM-09	RECORDS MANAGEMENT	LEG-07-03	Leases
ADM-09-02	Retention Schedule	MS	MARKETING & SALES
ADM-10	VENDORS	MS-01	CONTACT MANAGEMENT
ADM-11	CONSULTANTS	MS-04	MARKET RESEARCH
ADM-12	CONTRACTORS / SUBCONTRACTORS	MS-05	MARKET PLAN
ADM-14	PRESENTATION MATERIALS	MS-06	INDUSTRY COMPETITION
ADM-15	REFERENCE	MS-06-01	Press Clippings / Trade Articles
CR	CLIENT RELATIONS	MS-07	PROMOTIONS
CR-01	CLIENTS / ACCOUNTS	MS-08	PUBLIC RELATIONS / PUBLICITY
CR-02	PROJECTS / SPECIAL PROJECTS	MS-08-01	Newsletters
CR-03	COMPLAINTS	MS-08-02	Press Releases
FIN	FINANCE	MS-09	SALES
FIN-01	ASSETS	MS-09-01	Bids / Proposals
FIN-01-01	Fixed Assets	MS-09-04	Promotions
FIN-01-02	Depreciation	RR	REFERENCE / RESEARCH
FIN-02	AUDITS	RR-01	REFERENCE
FIN-02-02	External	RR-01-01	Industry
FIN-03	BANKING	RR-01-02	Management
FIN-03-01	Statements	RR-01-03	IT
FIN-03-05	Reconciliations	RR-02	RESEARCH & DEVELOPMENT
FIN-04	BUDGETS	RR-02-01	Technical Papers / References
		RR-03	STANDARDS

Hierarchical systems are common methods of arranging knowledge. The library classification system, Dewey Decimal, is a hierarchical system. Zoologists and botanists also use a hierarchical system to subdivide their subjects in descending order of *kingdom, phylum, superclass, class, order, family, subfamily, tribe, genus, species*, and so on.

Hierarchical arrangements are commonly used in filing systems because they limit the area of search. When subjects are arranged in straight alphabetic order, without regard for their subject relationship, searching requires scanning every single file folder caption. The use of a hierarchical category system focuses the search to a specific category. If a subject is not found in the most specific category, it will more than likely be found nearby, possibly in a more general category.

> When subjects are arranged in straight alphabetic order, without regard for their subject relationship, searching requires scanning every single file folder caption.

Grouping Functions

Categories are grouped according to the typical office function to which they relate. The subject categories you use will reflect the functions you perform in your business. Every function that produces records should be represented in your subject categories. Grouping the records by function improves the orderliness of the records.

When identifying your functions, do not confuse functions with departments. Functions do not always parallel departmental divisions. For example, your accounting department personnel may deal with administrative and information technology (IT) functions in addition to the standard accounting functions. The combination of functions is more obvious in a small business where fewer departmental divisions are identified.

> When identifying your functions, do not confuse functions with departments.

Number of Categories

Try to find a reasonable balance between the number of categories or subcategories and the volume of records. If the volume of records is moderately small, the subject categories should be broad and few. As the quantity increases, so does the need for more numerous and precise categories.

Try not to overcategorize your records. An excessive number of categories (subjects) or subcategories can create a serious filing problem. It can lead to overlapping files, making categorizing documents difficult. If categories are too highly specialized, you may find documents for which no appropriate filing place is available.

On the other hand, if categories or subcategories are too broad, you may have meaningless catch-all categories. Additional breakdowns may be necessary to better sort the records.

The terms you use or how you caption the categories or subcategories is a key influence on the number of categories you will have in your filing system. Certain modifiers can make the categories too restrictive. For example, AUTOMOBILE REPAIRS may be a good primary category. However, if the records sometimes concern other matters relating to automobiles, the word *repairs* is too restrictive. The broader term AUTOMOBILES, with an option of secondary categories, is a better subject caption. When choosing a term for a caption, make sure the caption mirrors the ways in which the records will be requested (i.e., terms used). Select terms you are comfortable using in your work environment. For example, you may find that CLIENT LIST is a more commonly used phrase than CONTACT MANAGEMENT.

Different businesses refer to similar documents by different names. For example, when requesting approval for a capital purchase, one business may use a *request for purchase (RFP)* form, while another business uses an *appropriation for expenditure (AFE)* form.

A business may gradually evolve unique acronyms or trade talk. If the use of a term clearly expresses its meaning, then you may use it as a category caption. The definition or the spelled-out term should be included within the category description to cross-reference the meaning of the term. For example, the term *G & A* may be more common than its definition, *General & Administrative Expenses*.

Coding the Categories

Category codes serve a couple of purposes. Primarily, they provide an abbreviated form of the category caption. When coding a document for filing, writing ACC-02-01 on the document is much easier than writing *Accounts Receivable, Billing/Invoices.* Secondarily, codes also help when sorting and filing because codes are easier to sort than long subject captions.

Alphabetic abbreviations for the categories may be adjusted to make them easier to remember. For example, you may use either AC or ACC to suggest ACCOUNTING; CO or COR to suggest CORPORATE; or CR or CLI to suggest CLIENT RELATIONS. Figure 6.3 demonstrates two different coding system alternatives.

Arrange Folders Within a Category

Each category contains large collections of related folders. To manage these folders, you must determine the appropriate folder arrangement. Within each individual category, files are arranged in an order best suited for rapid retrieval and disposition.

A specific feature or characteristic of the category is chosen as the basis for the arrangement. This characteristic is most easily identified by determining how various types of records are requested. Features may include a subject, a name associated with the record, a number that identifies the record, or a title. Using an existing feature is better than creating something at random. The most common filing arrangements are alphabetic, chronologic or date, geographic, and numeric.

Alphabetic Arrangement

In the **alphabetic filing arrangement**, records or entries are arranged in alphabetic order. Arranging records in alphabetic order is most helpful when records are retrieved by name or topic. However, even the simplest alphabetic system requires establishing consistent and uniform filing standards.

Figure 6.3

Alphanumeric and Duplex-Numeric Coding Systems

Coding System Alternatives			
Alphanumeric. This coding system is a combination of letters and numbers. Major subjects are encoded with a mnemonic abbreviation that suggests the subject. Subcategories are arranged in numeric or alphanumeric outline codes, separated by a dash, period, or space.			
ACC	ACCOUNTING	AC	ACCOUNTING
ACC-01	ACCOUNTS PAYABLE	AC 1	ACCOUNTS PAYABLE
ACC-01-01	Invoices	AC 1.a	Invoices
ACC-01-02	Expense Accounts	AC 1.b	Expense Accounts
Duplex-numeric. This coding system uses two or more sets of numbers. The parts are separated by a dash, space, comma, or period. Each subject is assigned a numeric code.			
01	ACCOUNTING	1	ACCOUNTING
01-01	ACCOUNTS PAYABLE	1-1	ACCOUNTS PAYABLE
01-01.01	Invoices	1-1.1	Invoices
01-01.02	Expense Accounts	1-1.2	Expense Accounts

Alphabetic filing systems use either the *dictionary arrangement* or the *encyclopedic arrangement*. The **dictionary arrangement** is a single alphabetic filing arrangement in which all types of entries (names, subjects, titles, etc.) are interfiled. In a dictionary system, folders are filed in straight alphabetic sequence, similar to the way words are ordered in a dictionary. See Figure 6.4.

The **encyclopedic arrangement** is an arrangement in which records are filed under broad, major headings (categories) and then under the specific subheading (subcategory) to which they relate. Headings and subheadings are arranged alphabetically. In the encyclopedic system shown in Figure 6.5, folders are grouped first by a topic or subject, then they are filed in straight alphabetic sequence within each topic. For example, when filing vendor information, you may first group vendors by product or service—the subheadings.

Chronologic or Date Arrangement

In a **chronologic filing arrangement**, records are arranged according to their dates, as shown in Figure 6.6. In a chronologic system, folders are arranged in sequential date order, using either numeric dates (07-01-02) or alphanumeric dates (July 1, 2002, 01-July-02, 2002-July-01, etc.). A chronologic filing system is used for logs or items that require daily reading such as scientific readings, weather, or cash flow. Chronologic files may also be used as "tickler" or reminder files. Use this arrangement sparingly, as remembering the "date of occurrence" is not an effective retrieval tool. You must also decide on a date format standard. For example, don't write out the month (July 1, 2002) on one folder and numerically annotate the month (07/01/02) on another folder.

Geographic Arrangement

Records filed in the **geographic filing arrangement** are arranged by geographic location, and they are usually arranged by numeric code or in alphabetic order. Grouping subjects together

Figure 6.4

Dictionary Filing Arrangement

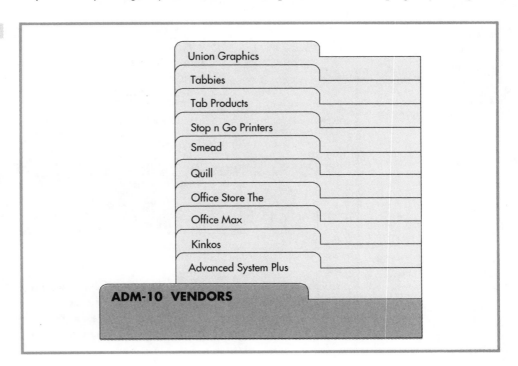

Union Graphics
Tabbies
Tab Products
Stop n Go Printers
Smead
Quill
Office Store The
Office Max
Kinkos
Advanced System Plus

ADM-10 VENDORS

Encyclopedic Filing Arrangement

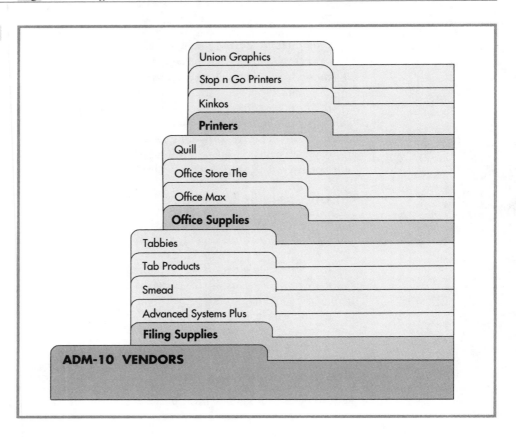

Chronologic Filing Arrangement

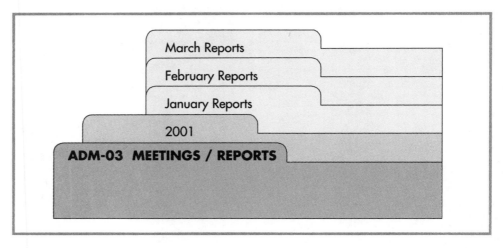

alphabetically by their physical locations is useful when filing records related to sales territories. Geographic folders can be filed in a dictionary arrangement, or they can be grouped in a logical topical arrangement by country, region, state, city, town, direction, etc. File users must know the location of correspondents or an index is needed to access the files. See Figure 6.7.

Figure 6.7

Geographic Filing Arrangement

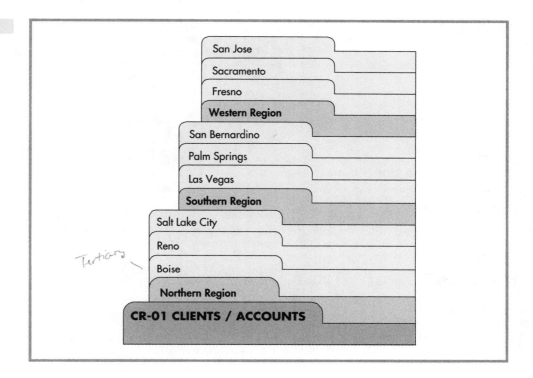

Tertiary

San Jose
Sacramento
Fresno
Western Region
San Bernardino
Palm Springs
Las Vegas
Southern Region
Salt Lake City
Reno
Boise
Northern Region
CR-01 CLIENTS / ACCOUNTS

Numeric Arrangement

In the **numeric filing arrangement,** records are filed in numeric order. Any classification system for arranging records that is based on numbers is a numeric arrangement. If folder contents are connected to a logical number and the information is normally retrieved by this number, then using this number for sequencing is appropriate. Examples include case numbers, customer numbers, addresses, purchase order numbers, batch numbers, lot numbers, etc. Numeric is the easiest kind of file arrangement to manage. Numbers are easy to remember, and fewer misfiles occur in a numeric system than in an alphabetic system. See Figure 6.8.

Use Alphabetic Filing Rules

A set of alphabetic filing rules provides the standards for consistent filing, which results in consistent, accurate retrieval of records.

To be successful, a system needs consistency and uniformity. A set of alphabetic filing rules provides the standards for consistent filing, which results in consistent, accurate retrieval of records. Conventional wisdom states that if you know the alphabet, you know how to file. Unfortunately, filing is not quite that easy. Alphabetic filing of some names may be interpreted in many different ways, and the details of how to arrange unusual names can be confusing. Establishing and adhering to filing rules promotes filing consistency and retrieval reliability.

Standard alphabetic rules are available from ARMA International. The rules presented here are based on these standards.

1. Alphabetize by arranging files in unit-by-unit (or word-by-word) order and letter by letter within each unit.

2. Consider each filing unit or word in a filing segment. A unit includes prepositions, conjunctions, and articles. The word "the" is the last filing unit in a filing segment. Symbols (&, $, #) are spelled out and filed alphabetically.

Figure 6.8

Numeric Filing Arrangement

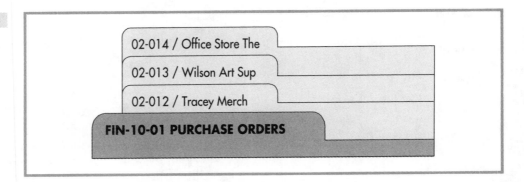

3. File "nothing before something." For example, file Brown before Browne. File single unit segments before multiple unit segments. For example, file Expressions before Expressions Deluxe.

4. Ignore all punctuation when alphabetizing. Punctuation includes periods, commas, dashes, hyphens, apostrophes, etc. Hyphenated words are considered one unit.

5. Arabic and Roman numbers are filed sequentially before alphabetic characters. All Arabic numbers precede all Roman numerals.

6. Acronyms, abbreviations, and radio and television station call letters are filed as one unit.

7. File under the most commonly used name. Cross-reference under other names or titles that might be used in an information request.

Personal Names

Use the last name (surname) as the first filing unit. The first name or initial is the second unit. Subsequent names or initials are filed as subsequent units.

Names	Names as Filed by Unit		
As Written	1st Unit	2d Unit	3d Unit
H. Daniel Hiatt	Hiatt	H	Daniel
Sharon K. Signori	Signori	Sharon	K
Danny Lee Taylor	Taylor	Danny	Lee

Ignore hyphens and file the two words as one unit. Surnames that include a prefix are filed as one unit whether the prefix is followed by a space or punctuation or not.

As Written	1st Unit	2d Unit	3d Unit
Bruno Della Rosa	Della Rosa	Bruno	
Jonathan Garey-Sage	GareySage	Jonathan	
Monica MacGreggor	MacGreggor	Monica	
Kathleen M. St. Peter	StPeter	Kathleen	M

When needed to distinguish between two or more identical names, titles and suffixes are the last filing units and are filed as written, ignoring punctuation.

As Written	1st Unit	2d Unit	3d Unit
Father Frank O'Shay	OShay	Frank	Father
Wendel Torres, Jr.	Torres	Wendel	Jr
Dr. Jamie Walters	Walters	Jamie	Dr

Business Names

A business name is filed as written, even when it contains the name of an individual, using the complete name of the business.

Names	Names as Filed by Unit			
As Written	1st Unit	2d Unit	3d Unit	4th Unit
The Crab House	Crab	House	The	
Reno Bicycle Co.	Reno	Bicycle	Co	
Ted Young's Cafe	Ted	Youngs	Cafe	
Webster West, Inc.	Webster	West	Inc	

All punctuation, such as commas, dashes, periods, hyphens, and apostrophes are ignored, and names are indexed as written. Articles, conjunctions, and prepositions are separate filing units. The word "The" is the last filing unit. Symbols are spelled out.

As Written	1st Unit	2d Unit	3d Unit	4th Unit
Col-R-Tab	ColRTab			
Knock-on-Wood Shop	KnockOnWood	Shop		
Let's Dance Studio	Lets	Dance	Studio	
Rick & Billy Pizza	Rick	and	Billy	Pizza
Robert's Equestrian Center	Roberts	Equestrian	Center	

Single letters, acronyms, abbreviations, and radio and television station call letters are filed as a single filing unit. Disregard any punctuation marks, ampersands, or spaces used with such letters.

As Written	1st Unit	2d Unit	3d Unit	4th Unit
K&B Furniture	KB	Furniture		
KEYZ Radio	KEYZ	Radio		

Names with numbers written as digits in the first unit precede all alphabetic names. Arabic numbers precede Roman numerals. Disregard any st or th endings on numbers.

As Written	1st Unit	2d Unit	3d Unit	4th Unit
5 Star Energy Co.	5	Star	Energy	Co
17th Street Gym	17	Street	Gym	
After 5 Lounge	After	5	Lounge	
Two Dollar Store	Two	Dollar	Store	

Government Names

The name of the major entity (country, state, province) is filed first, followed by the distinctive name of the department or bureau, etc., reversing the written order where necessary to give the distinctive name precedence in the filing arrangement.

Names	Names as Filed by Unit			
As Written	1st Unit	2d Unit	3d Unit	4th Unit
Department of Education, Colorado	Colorado	Education	Department of	
Department of Agriculture	US	Agriculture	Department of	

Foreign Governments   File by the formal name of the government. Cross-reference the written English name to the official native name where necessary.

Names		Names as Filed by Unit		
As Written	1st Unit	2d Unit	3d Unit	4th Unit
Commonwealth of Australia	Commonwealth	of	Australia	
Republic of China (Taiwan)	Republic	of	China	

Chapter 7

Storage Solutions

Who would have thought so many trendy new products for office storage would be available? More and more merchants are selling organizing and storage solutions for small and home-based businesses. Big-box office supply stores, such as *OfficeMax*, *Staples*, and *Office Depot*, are commonplace in every city. Even stores commonly thought of as domestic stores, such as *Crate and Barrel*, *The Container Store*, and *Target*, are selling office organizing and storage solutions. Moreover, if you can't find the storage solution you are looking for in a brick-and-mortar store, you can find it on the Internet.

Smaller offices can take advantage of these storage and organization products available in many popular stores. However, you must look to your long-term objectives. Most big businesses were once small businesses. Visualize where you will be in five years or ten years. Before you buy any new storage product, think through its form and functionality. Is it purely decorative or does it actually fit your overall, long-term storage plan?

Storage Plan

One of the quickest ways to reduce the efficiency of any workspace is failing to properly consider storage needs.

Your storage plan identifies storage products best suited for your documents and your office space. One of the quickest ways to reduce the efficiency of any workspace is failing to properly consider storage needs. Before you purchase any products, you must first identify your needs. To understand your storage needs, answering the following questions will provide a strong basis for making purchasing decisions.

1. *Equipment capacity*

   - *How many linear inches of filing do you have? What is your current capacity?* Filing is measured in linear inches. A linear inch is a measurement of length; so to determine your current volume, use a yardstick or a measuring tape to measure total linear filing inches.

   - *How do you determine the filing capacity of filing equipment?* Measure the linear filing space within the equipment, then subtract at least 10 percent for working space (i.e., wiggle room). For example, the filing capacity of a standard vertical, 4-drawer, 25-inch-deep file cabinet is 90 linear inches.

2. *Growth expectations*

- *What are your growth expectations for the records? Do you know how many records you may be adding in a year or two?* If you are maintaining your active records appropriately and are cycling out inactive or obsolete records, you can still expect to grow by at least 20 to 25 percent a year.

3. *Space limitations*

- *Do you have limited office floor space available for filing equipment?* To determine floor space for a piece of equipment, add the measurements of the cabinet footprint, the drawer pull-out space, and access space (i.e., standing room). When measuring from the wall, a standard 4-drawer vertical file cabinet requires at least 6 feet or more of floor space:

       28-inch cabinet footprint
       + 28-inch pull-out drawer
       + 18-inch access space
       = 74 inches (6 feet, 2 inches) of linear floor space

  If floor space is an issue, consider installing open-face shelving units that maximize the available floor space.

- *What are the constraints of the available space?* Consider multipurpose equipment such as shelving units that double as space dividers or a lateral filing cabinet with a work surface on top.

4. *Simultaneous use*

- *How many users access the filing equipment simultaneously?* If the files are accessed by more than one user at a time, consider an open-shelving unit instead of a closed-drawer cabinet.

5. *Compatibility with materials*

- *Do you have a letter-size or legal-size equipment standard?* Costs of legal-size equipment and supplies can be 20 to 30 percent higher than for letter size. A typical office stores very few legal-size documents. If most of your records are letter-size, then consider a letter-size filing standard.

- *Do you keep oversize materials such as drawings, maps, charts, or plans?* Consider specialty equipment designed to store oversized materials such as hanging files, flat files, or tube files.

- *Do you also store an assorted array of media, including index cards, videotapes, diskettes, and CDs?* Select a mixed-media cabinet that can be equipped to fit a variety of media types.

6. *Protection requirements*

- *Are you storing confidential records?* Locks are needed to safeguard the contents of storage equipment.

- *Are the records irreplaceable?* Fire-resistant cabinets or vaults are needed to safeguard vital records.

7. *Accessibility*

- *Are storage units too high for users?* Auxiliary equipment, such as stools or safety ladders, may be purchased to improve access to higher shelves.

● *Do users need to access equipment while sitting?* Several motorized options can be operated while the user is sitting, such as power files with shelves that rotate vertically, much like a Ferris wheel. Although very expensive, power files are compliant with the Americans with Disabilities Act (ADA) and may be justified for businesses with disabled employees.

Filing Equipment

What kind of equipment do you need? What type of storage would be most effective? Such needs may vary widely, and you should assess them individually rather than using a cookie-cutter approach.

Filing equipment is available in an assortment of sizes, shapes, and price ranges. Finding the configuration that best meets your needs requires careful selection. We are accustomed to seeing the standard four-drawer vertical file cabinet. Although these cabinets are inexpensive and abundant, other storage equipment configurations may be better suited to your needs.

Equipment designs include vertical and lateral file-drawer cabinets, open-shelf units, mechanical units, and specialty filing units.

File Cabinets

Drawer file cabinets designed for top-tab folders are suitable for documents requiring extra protection. The top-tab format permits drop-in filing—documents can be conveniently dropped into a folder without removing it from a drawer.

Locks on these cabinets are generally not of sufficient quality to provide much security, but they can provide controlled access. File cabinets are most suitable for personal offices and for records that are not accessed frequently.

Vertical Cabinets   The standard vertical file cabinet is the most commonly used file cabinet. These cabinets are manufactured in two- to five-drawer models in both letter- and legal-size. The quality and features of vertical cabinets will differ with each manufacturer. Some cabinets have a compressor built into the bottom of the drawer to hold folders upright. Some have high drawer sides for suspending folders, or you can insert a hanging-folder frame.

Vertical file cabinets in general require a large amount of floor space. You have to account for not only the cabinet, but also the aisle space needed in front of every cabinet for users to pull out drawers. For example, a 28-inch-deep cabinet needs 46 inches of aisle space to allow for drawer pullout plus access space.

Lateral Cabinets   A lateral file cabinet is similar to a standard filing cabinet except the drawers open on the long side as shown in Figure 7.1. Standard widths for lateral cabinets are 30, 36, and 42 inches for both letter and legal size. Lateral file cabinets will hold standing folders or suspended folders. The typical filing format is side-to-side; however, some manufactures provide a front-to-back filing option.

Lateral cabinets have a much larger filing capacity and occupy less floor space than standard vertical cabinets. The cost of lateral cabinets, however, is generally greater per filing inch than either vertical cabinets or shelves.

Open-Shelf Storage Units

Open-shelf filing systems store records on open horizontal shelves, rather than in drawers, leaving all folders visible with direct access to the records. Standard shelving widths, for both letter- and legal-size units, are 36, 42, and 48 inches. Shelving unit quality and features will

Figure 7.1

Lateral File Cabinets
(Courtesy: Spacesaver
Corporation)

Figure 7.2

**Open-Shelf and Mixed-
Media Storage Unit**
(Courtesy: Spacesaver
Corporation)

vary with each manufacturer. In some units, shelves can be interchanged with mixed-media containers, allowing for a very versatile filing system.

To restrict access to records, doors can be added to some units. The style of door—tambour, flipper, hinged, and sliding—will vary by manufacturer. See Figure 7.2, which shows open shelves with doors on the top and mixed-media drawers on the lower half of the cabinet.

File folders are stored with side tabs facing out, which makes an excellent stage for a color-coded filing system. Color coding the folder tabs adds to increased accuracy in filing and retrieving folders.

Open-shelf file units are the most space efficient of all available filing equipment. These units occupy less than 50 percent of the floor space required for standard vertical file cabinets. Because the units are open-faced, aisle space needed for these units is minimal. They can provide answers to problems originating from rising file costs, lack of office space, and file retrieval difficulties. A disadvantage of an open system is that records may be vulnerable to fire or unauthorized access.

Mechanized Storage Units

Mechanized units are filing units in which files are moved either manually or by a motor for easy access. These units are designed for high-density filing where the volume of records exceeds the available floor space. Although some of these units can be fairly expensive, units that are suitable, as well as affordable, are available for small businesses.

Shelving Units on Glider Tracks   This type of system allows shelving units to be stacked in rows two or three deep without the need for aisle space between rows. The units in the back row are stationary, and the units in front are individually mounted onto glider tracks that are imbedded into a platform. The units glide laterally along these tracks. To access the back units, you simply slide a front unit to the left or right, much like a sliding closet door, as shown in Figure 7.3. These systems may not be compatible for systems requiring high-access activity, i.e., multiple users requiring simultaneous access.

Figure 7.3

Bi-File
(Courtesy: Spacesaver
Corporation)

Pull-Out Units Pull-out units are single-faced shelving units that are stacked next to one another, much like books on a shelf. To access records, pull the unit out from the shelving stack in a straight linear motion. The units move without the use of tracks or rail system. These units are more efficient than the glider units because they allow multiple, simultaneous file users. See Figure 7.4.

Double-Faced Revolving Units These rotary shelf units consist of a three-sided open cabinet that contains a double-faced shelving unit inside the cabinet. The internal shelving unit is on a center pivot that permits the unit to turn or rotate inside the cabinet. Users turn the shelf unit manually or by pressing a button to turn the unit to access records on one side. They turn the shelf again to access records on the other side. A mechanized rotary storage unit is shown in Figure 7.5. These shelf units have two filing sides and two wall sides. When the shelf unit is turned so that a wall side faces the opening, the unit is in the closed postion. From this position the unit can be locked to restrict file access.

Figure 7.4

QuickSpace™ Storage System
(Courtesy: SpaceSaver
Corporation)

These storage units are very versatile. They can be placed against a wall or used as a room divider. Counter-height units can be used as worktables. The shelves can be interchanged for mixed-media storage components as well.

Specialty Filing Units

Manufacturers have designed filing equipment for many special types and styles of media. Storage equipment is available for any type of media and for oversize documents. Fire-resistant units are also available for special storage situations.

Mixed-Media Storage A mixed-media storage unit, shown in Figure 7.6, is designed to store a variety of media types such as optical disks, CD-ROMs, diskettes, magnetic tapes, videotapes, binders, etc. Although media drawer cabinets are available, the most versatile storage units for small volumes of various media are units that accept interchangeable media components.

Oversize Document Storage Oversize documents, such as plans, maps, drawings, blueprints, etc., require specialized filing containers such as flat files (shown in Figure 7.7), hanging files, and rolled files. Flat files store documents in wide, shallow drawers or in less expensive stack trays. Hanging files suspend documents by clipping them to a rod attached to a wall or a stand. Rolled files are designed for high-density, inactive storage. Documents are rolled and stored in tubes or in pigeonhole compartments within corrugated fiberboard boxes.

Fire-Resistant Units The ability of fire-resistant storage units to withstand fire damage is based on standardized ratings. These ratings specify the temperatures they can withstand and the length of time they can withstand them before damage begins to occur. Units designed for paper storage will not adequately protect electronic media. Electronic media, such as diskettes, CDs, and magnetic tapes, can tolerate neither the higher temperatures nor the humidity levels found in paper-rated products. When selecting fire-resistant storage units, be sure you understand the rating for the units and make your selection based on the media it will contain.

Space Planning

> The goal is an office area that encourages efficiency as well as comfort.

Space planning coordinates the environmental attributes of an office—structural design, electrical sources, light sources, and traffic flow—with the material assets such as furniture, workstations, and equipment. The goal is an office area that encourages efficiency as well as comfort.

Begin preparing your office plan by mapping the space available. Include space for equipment and filing areas.

Space Mapping

The first step is to sketch a floor plan of the office area, see Figure 7.8. The drawing can be done on graph paper with a pencil and ruler or with graphic software such as MS Visio. Note the location of all walls, partitions, support columns, doors (and the space to open the doors), and windows. Also, note the location of all wall switches, electrical outlets, telephone jacks, and network jacks.

Next, measure your furniture and workstations, and all office equipment. Sketch these items on a different piece of paper, using the same scale as your floor plan. Cut out the sketches and use them to approximate the best layout by placing them onto your floor plan.

Note the movement through the office. Chart the typical traffic paths, such as to the door, rest room, elevator, closets, hallways, etc. Gauge about five feet for main aisles or walkways and at least three feet for side aisles. Make allowances for drawer pullouts, door openings, chair movement, and cabinet door openings.

Consider frequency of use. Items used daily or weekly should be placed in easily accessible locations. Items used less frequently, such as monthly or yearly, should be stored in less active areas such as closets, cupboards, or storage areas.

Figure 7.7

Oversize Document File (Flat File)
(Courtesy: SpaceSaver Corporation)

Equipment Space

For every piece of equipment you place into your office, an accepted task will accompany it. When designing your space, create an Equipment List (see Figure 7.9). List all equipment you will be locating in the space. Identify the tasks associated with each piece of equipment and note any additional space needed for performing the tasks. Also, consider areas for storing equipment supplies, such as paper, printer cartridges, etc., and additional task-related materials.

Keep this list in mind when planning your space. By clustering equipment with

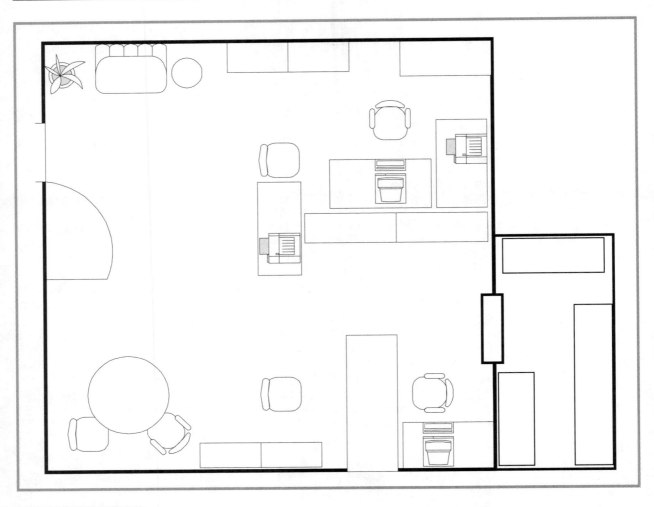

Figure 7.8

Sample Space Map

supplies and good working space, you keep everything within easy reach. Completing a task at its source is more efficient.

For example, how often have you used a copy machine that had no adjacent work-space? After copying, you wandered around with an armload of papers, looking for a place to collate your documents. If you were lucky, you found a clear space; otherwise, you had to set everything down while you shoved other papers aside. Or, if you were really pressed for time, you would just collate right on top of an already cluttered area. Then you had to trot back to your desk for a stapler or paper punch and dig through a couple of storage cabinets to find matching report covers, and on and on. How much time did you take to accomplish a simple collating task? Instead, take a tip from your local Kinko's. Adjacent to the machine is a counter-height work area for sorting and collating. The area is well stocked with most of the necessary supplies such as staplers, paper cutters, paper punches, pens, paper clips, etc. Also nearby (for staff use only) is ample storage for additional paper and ink-cartridge storage.

Equipment List

Equipment	Tasks	Supplies	Space
Copier	Collating, sorting, stapling	Print cartridge, reams of paper, stapler, staple remover, pens, paper punch	Work, storage
Departmental file	Sorting, filing, referencing	Out cards, file dividers, in-box, refile box, paper punch	Reference, storage
Fax machine	Collating, sorting, stapling	Print cartridge, reams of paper, stapler, staple remover, pens, fax cover sheets	Work, storage
Network printer	Collating, sorting, stapling	Print cartridge, reams of paper, stapler, paper punch	Work, storage
Personal file cabinet	Filing, referencing	Folders, hanging folders, index tabs	Reference, storage
Personal printers - 2		Print cartridge, reams of paper	Storage

Figure 7.9

Sample Equipment List

File Areas

File areas are used for *personal files* or *central files*. Personal files are the very active files generally located within an individual's workstation. Central files are the active files placed within central or common areas of the office.

- **Personal files.** A personal file area is within an arm's reach of a person's workstation such as desk-drawer files, over-the-desk shelves, credenzas, bookcases, etc.

  Resist the temptation to create a large amount of personal file storage space. This area should contain only very **active records**, i.e., records used on a daily basis. Materials tend to fill the space allowed. If space is provided, it is quickly filled and rarely referenced. Typically, important records are found on top of the desk while old, outdated documents consume all the storage space.

- **Central files.** Central files contain active records (current year) and some semiactive records (past year or two). These files can be configured for the whole office or grouped by department. Usually, this configuration consists of banks of file cabinets or rows of file shelving. This type of arrangement may not work if space is limited or if primary users cannot easily access the area. In this case, filing units may be separated and functionally clustered around work groups. No right or wrong way exists for clustering the storage units. The layout is dependent on the most efficient arrangement for users.

Configure your file areas in a manner that will promote efficiency as well as maximize available space. When you are placing storage units, consider frequency of use. Frequently used records should be stored in locations that are easily accessible. Less frequently used records can be moved to a less accessible area. **Inactive records** (infrequently used), such as the records that are seldom referenced but are kept to comply with your retention schedule, should not be stored in the office at all. These records should be stored in out-of-the-way or off-site areas.

Analyze your filing and storage needs and select filing units that will meet these needs. Configure your area for its maximum filing capacity. Additional considerations include:

- Keep the plan flexible.
- Provide room for 20 to 25 percent annual growth.
- Provide a reference or file preparation area.
- Provide space for "to-be-filed" and "to-be-refiled" collections.
- Establish standards in equipment style for the entire office.

File equipment vendors can be excellent sources of help with filing area layouts for small businesses. Vendors can help you determine file volume, assess your space, and offer suggestions for space planning. To find a vendor in your area, check your *Yellow Pages'* index for *filing equipment systems and supplies* or check the *Buyer's Guide* on ARMA International's Web site at www.arma.org for records management supplies.

The layout of the file area will depend on the volume of records you are storing and the function and style of equipment you have selected. Figure 7.10 shows a 16-foot wall and the different equipment styles and configurations that can fit along this wall. This sample layout illustrates the effect that equipment style has on filing capacity. Although the area remains static, the capacity can be drastically adjusted with higher-density systems.

Figure 7.10

File Area Layout

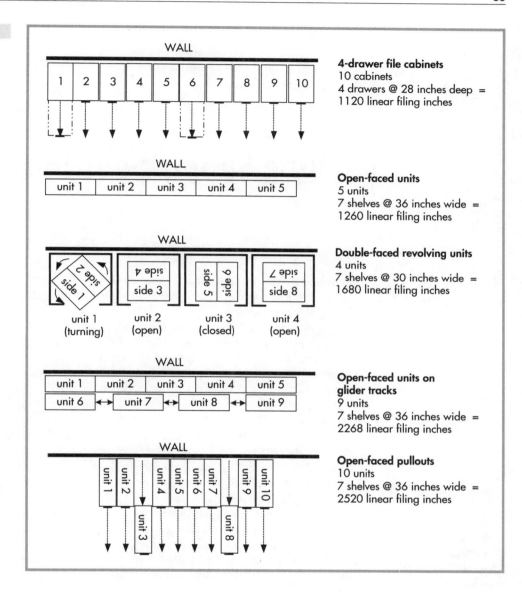

4-drawer file cabinets
10 cabinets
4 drawers @ 28 inches deep =
1120 linear filing inches

Open-faced units
5 units
7 shelves @ 36 inches wide =
1260 linear filing inches

Double-faced revolving units
4 units
7 shelves @ 30 inches wide =
1680 linear filing inches

Open-faced units on glider tracks
9 units
7 shelves @ 36 inches wide =
2268 linear filing inches

Open-faced pullouts
10 units
7 shelves @ 36 inches wide =
2520 linear filing inches

Filing Supply Solutions

The final part in the preparation of your filing system is determining the filing supplies you will need. Filing supplies include the guides, file folders, and labels that help users locate records and information.

Beginning in the Middle Ages and for several centuries following, filing meant spindling documents onto thin spike-like wires. In the mid-nineteenth century, filing systems evolved into storing documents in flat boxes or drawers. Thirty years after the invention of the typewriter, in 1892, Dr. Nathan Rosenau hit on the idea of filing documents vertically, the same way that he filed index cards. By the early twentieth century, the idea had gained universal popularity, and the era of the file folder and file cabinet had begun.

In the late 1970s and early 1980s, futurists began talking about the demise of paper documents and the advent of the paperless office. The office of the future was to be a workplace filled with the best technology had to offer and the promise of more sophisticated automation to come. We fully expected our file cabinets and file folders to finally become obsolete.

Something went terribly wrong along the way. The digital age has created more paper, not less. Experts have estimated that over 90 percent of all office documents are retained on paper.[1,2,3] According to industry experts, over the last twenty years, office paper consumption has steadily increased, and no slowdown in consumption is expected.[4]

Unfortunately, a new, magical product to store paper isn't available. As we have for the last 80 years, we put paper into file folders and file them. Instead of file folders becoming office novelties, as once predicted, we are buying more folders than ever, because we still need to put all this paper somewhere.

In a worst-case scenerio, office workers can spend, on average, over three hours a week looking for missing or misplaced papers.[5,6] Because time is money, a small business owner can little afford this search time. With so much paper and so little time, an efficient filing system is essential to the ability to file and retrieve information. The right filing supplies can make a difference and can eliminate many problems that afflict inadequate filing systems.

> The right filing supplies can make a difference and can eliminate many problems that afflict inadequate filing systems.

File Folders

File folders are available in two types: top tab and side tab. Top-tab folders are used in drawer files; side-tab folders are used in open-shelf files. File folders are manufactured in a variety of materials and styles. Knowing and understanding these variations will prepare you for purchasing folders that meet your specific requirements.

Stiffness and Durability

The activity level of folders is an important consideration. The more active the folder, the sturdier the folder construction should be. For most applications, a standard, reinforced-tab manila folder will work quite well. Thicker files may require a heavy-duty folder such as one made with pressboard or an expanding file pocket folder.

Folder paper stock is available in several thicknesses or points. A folder having a higher point value is more rigid and more durable. Documents stored in a less stiff folder may curl and sag towards the bottom

File Folder Point Values	
9.5 pt. Manila	17 pt. Manila or Kraft (unbleached)
11 pt. Manila	20 pt. Classification or Pressboard
14 pt. Manila	25 pt. Pressboard

of the folder. As a rule, the more paper stored in a folder, the higher the point value of the folder should be.

Tabs

A **tab** is a projection on the top or side of a folder. A label with a caption, identifying the folder contents, is normally affixed to the tab. The manufacturer may strengthen the tab by adding a double layer of material along the edge of the tab.

Folders are manufactured in a variety of tab positions. The most common is the one-third-cut position; however, the most versatile is the straight-cut position (for top-tab filing) or full-cut position (for side-tab filing). A straight-cut tab runs the full length of a folder. For ease of reference, always place the folder label in a uniform position on all folder tabs.

Do not randomly stagger one-third-cut tabs when arranging folders in file drawers. Instead, align the folder tabs with your category-coding scheme. The eye sees in straight lines, and filing is much more efficient if the tabs follow a straight line in the drawer.

Codes are assigned to the file categories. The code is broken into three parts: the letters, which identify the major category, the first two numbers, which identify the primary category, and the last two numbers, which identify the secondary category. Each tab position is assigned to part of the code as shown in Figure 8.1. The first position is assigned to the major category; second position is assigned to the primary category; and third position is assigned to the secondary category.

One-third-cut folders are sold in boxes with an equal number of folders in each tab position. With this filing arrangement, you will need more right-tab (third position) folders than left-tab (first position) or middle-tab folders (second position). You can partially solve this dilemma by turning the left-tab folder inside-out and making it a right tab.

Top Tab   Top-tab folders are used in filing drawers. The most commonly used tab types are:

- *Straight cut.* The top tab runs the full length of the folder.
- *One-third cut.* The top-tab length is 1/3 the length of the folder.
- *One-fifth cut.* The top-tab length is 1/5 the length of the folder.

Side Tab   Side-tab folders (also known as *end-tab folders*) are designed for shelf filing. Side-tab folders are very popular because of their high-density filing capacity and color-coding capabilities. Some commonly used side-tab folders are:

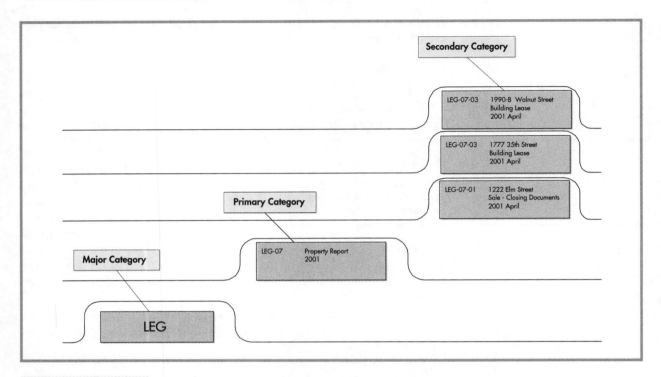

Figure 8.1

One-Third-Cut Tab Positions

- *Full cut.* The side tab runs the full length of the folder side.
- *Undercut* or *notched cut.* The bottom of the tab is notched. This type of folder is used in cabinet shelves that have a lip.
- *Four-inch tab lower position.* Only the bottom four inches of the folder has a tab. These folders are used with index guides whose tabs are displayed in the upper four inches.

Special Folder Styles

Folders are manufactured in many different styles for many different uses and are available in letter or legal sizes.

Classification A **classification folder** is a heavy-duty pressboard folder with one or two inner dividers. The folder has fasteners on the front and back covers and double-faced fasteners on each divider. It provides four or six places to separate and file documents within one folder.

Combination Drawer / Shelf **Combination folders** have both a top tab, for drawer files, and a side tab, for open-shelf files.

Expandable Pocket A **pocket folder** is a partially enclosed folder with side-panel gussets for expansion. They are manufactured in different styles and materials. Some pocket folders have accordion-pleat gussets so that pockets can easily expand to hold numerous papers and documents. Expansions can range from 3/4 inches to as wide as 5 inches.

Hanging Folders A **hanging folder** has small hooks on each corner that allow it to be hung on or suspended from a frame. These folders are used to hold loose documents, odd-size documents, bound documents, etc. They are ideal for small filing areas such as desk or credenza drawers. Hanging folders have plastic tabs that can be inserted into any position along the long-side of the folder. Captions are written or keyed onto labels that are inserted into the plastic tabs.

Jacket   A **jacket folder** is a flat folder that is closed on three sides. It is used to hold odd-size documents, bound documents, loose documents, brochures, etc.

Folder Features

Folders are available with special features that meet a variety of applications.

Color   Folders are available in colors that vary by manufacturer. Color folders allow you to color code your filing system for improved filing and retrieval. When you assign different colors to different filing categories, file users soon learn the colors used for the categories. They know immediately where to file a folder, and they can quickly identify a misfiled folder.

Score Lines   Most folders are designed to expand. Manila folders have three scored or creased lines near the bottom or folded edge. Approximately 25 sheets of paper (1/4 inch) can be stored in the folder before bending or *scoring* the folder at the first score line. Scoring allows a folder to expand to a capacity of about 100 sheets of paper (3/4 inch). Scoring a folder will keep papers from protruding beyond the edge of the folder and covering the folder label, which slows storage and retrieval.

Fasteners   Prong fasteners can be bonded (glued) to or embedded (firmly attached with prongs) onto folders. These fasteners are used to secure documents to folders.

Inside Pocket   Some folders have an inside pocket. This inside pocket is designed to hold a CD, a 3.5-inch diskette, loose papers, smaller documents, etc.

Polyethylene   A polyethylene (poly) file folder is made of a durable vinyl-type material that repels moisture and resists tears. These folders are designed for very active files and are available in various styles.

Small business owners who buy in large quantities may find better prices and more options if they use a filing supply dealer. To find a vendor in your area, check your *Yellow Pages'* index for *filing equipment systems and supplies.* A vendor can assist with folder selection.

Cost Considerations

When planning your filing system, you also need to plan how you will store records into folders and the level of activity to which the folders will be subjected. This type of information will help you consider the cost implications of filing supplies you will need. You may make changes when you become aware of the costs involved.

Document Order   If document order is important, then folders with fasteners should be considered. Folders with factory mounted fasteners are more expensive. However, if the documents must be secured into the folder, this cost may be justified.

File Activity   Very active folders should be constructed of sturdier stock, but sturdier stock is also more expensive. If your folders are very active, the cost of pressboard folders may well be justified because manila stock may not be able to withstand the activity and may require periodic replacement. On the other hand, folders that are only occasionally referenced are well suited for less expensive manila stock.

Folder Colors   Colored file folders are more expensive than manila folders of the same weight and size. However, as noted previously, color-coded folders greatly improve storage and retrieval rates. Will the improved efficiency justify the extra cost?

Folder Size Legal-size folders are more expensive than letter-size folders. Additionally, few companies today use legal-size paper, which means that if you don't use legal-size paper and you don't correspond with other companies that use legal-size paper, you won't need legal-size folders.

Hanging Folders with Manila Folder Inserts A double filing system is frequently used to assign a "home" for the manila folder. When the manila folder is charged out (borrowed from the storage unit), the hanging folder keeps the folder space open. Although having a placeholder is an advantage, the downside is that it almost doubles the cost of supplies.

Internal Subgrouping If documents within a folder must be subgrouped in a specific manner, classification folders should be considered. For example, a contract file may have internal subgroups such as correspondence, notes, drafts, and final contract. In this instance, the cost of a classification folder may be justified as an alternative to individual folders that may become separated during use.

Large Hanging Folder Systems Not only are hanging folders more expensive than manila folders, hanging folders also take up much more filing space. In a storage unit full of hanging folders, the folders alone will consume a third of the space.

Labels

Most labels on the market today are adhesive, sheet labels designed for use with inkjet or laser printers. Labels are available in different sizes, colors, and formats. Labels may be white with a colored stripe or a solid color.

A label identifies the contents of a folder—the category code, the content title caption, and the year or inclusive dates, as appropriate. A standard laser printer label is shown in Figure 8.2; color-coded folder labels are shown in Figure 8.3.

Labels should be easy to read, precise, and complete. Information should be keyed onto the labels in a consistent fashion, and the labels should be affixed in a uniform, consistent position on all folder tabs.

Guides

As their name indicates, guides direct users to a specific location and serve as "signposts" to visually aid in filing and finding records. The orderly appearance and efficiency of the filing system depends upon proper use of guides.

Figure 8.2

Sample Laser Printer Folder Labels

LEG-01-01	2001
LOVELL & LOVELL CONTRACT – FEASIBILITY STUDY – 11/19/01 Final Contract	
LEG-01-01	2001
SIGNORI HIATT & WALTERS CONTRACT – FEASIBILITY STUDY – 12/01/01 Final Contract	

Figure 8.3
**Color-Coded Folder
Labels**

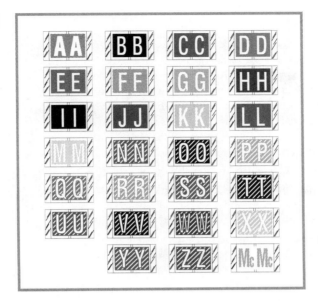

File Guides

Guides, shown in Figure 8.4, in file drawers or on file shelves are not only finding aids, but they also help keep folders standing erect. Materials used to construct guides, such as pressboard and plastic, are very rigid and sturdy. Note the straight-line arrangement of folders in third position with guides in first position. Using only one-third cut, third-position folders provides more efficient storage and retrieval. Users can make a faster visual check when folders are not in a staggered arrangement. One guide to about every ten folders is the accepted standard.

Figure 8.4

File Guides

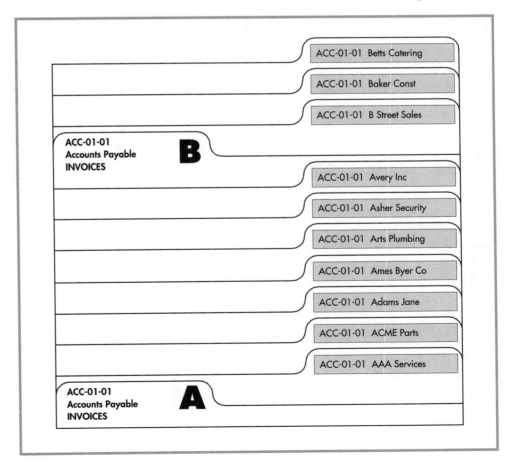

Out Guides

When a folder is removed from a drawer or shelf, an out guide replaces the borrowed folder and signals that the folder is charged out (removed or borrowed). Out guides are also made of sturdy material, the word OUT is printed on the tabs, and they are a distinctive color that allows users to quickly see where folders or other materials have been removed, as shown in Figure 8.5. When a borrowed file is returned, the out guide is removed, and the folder is returned to its original location. If multiple users have access to the files, these guides are very important for maintaining control over the stored records, as they help provide an accounting of where each folder is located at all times. Out guides are available in two commonly used types:

- A tabbed guide having preprinted lines for writing the borrower's name and the date on which the folder was removed. When the folder is returned, the borrower removes the out guide and crosses off his/her name. The out guide is then placed where the next borrower can use it.
- A tabbed guide on which vinyl pockets are attached. One plastic pocket is used for inserting a charge-out slip the borrower has filled out. A second, larger pocket is used for inserting documents that accumulate while the folder is charged out. When the folder is returned, the slip is removed and tossed, and any documents that have accumulated are filed in proper order in the folder.

Color Codes

We are accustomed to color-coded objects in our world. The color of a blanket lets us know whether a baby is a boy or a girl, the color of the spout lets us know whether the coffee in the pot is regular or decaf, and the color on faucet handles lets us know whether the water is hot or cold. Colored traffic lights show us when to stop, when to yield, and when to go.

In offices, color also serves as a visual aid for filing and finding operations. Colors help prevent misfiles, act as signals in disposition, and help identify folders on a desk. Colors can be used to visually distinguish one file category from another, one year from another, or one customer from another.

Colored Labels

Although the use of colored file folders is attractive, an easier method is to use solid color bars. With colored folders, you must maintain a large inventory of the colored folders you use most often. With color bar labels, you stock a box of 500 labels in each color. Using colored labels is less expensive and much more convenient. Assign a color to each major category, as shown in Figure 8.6.

Color bars will work with both top-tab and side-tab folders as shown in Figure 8.7. Always place the color bar label in a uniform position on tabs.

Start small. You may want to start with just one color, then add more labels, such as colored

Figure 8.5

Out Guide

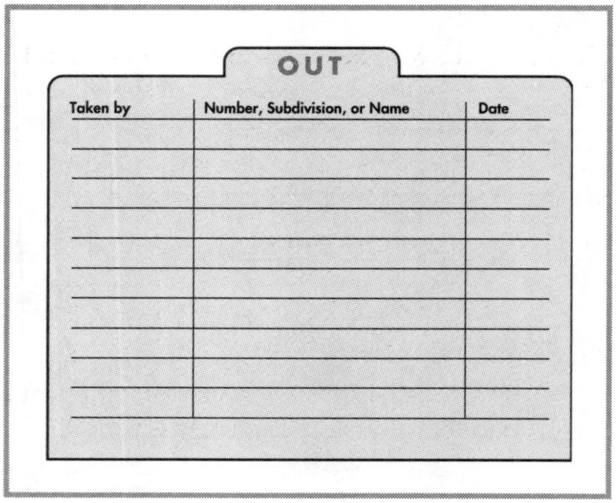

OUT		
Taken by	Number, Subdivision, or Name	Date

Colors help prevent misfiles, act as signals in disposition, and help identify folders on a desk.

Figure 8.6

Sample Category Color Codes

CODE	NAME	COLOR	
ACC	ACCOUNTING	Lt. Green	
ADM	ADMINISTRATION	Yellow	
CR	CLIENT RELATIONS	Dk. Blue	
COR	CORPORATE	Gray	
FIN	FINANCE	Dk. Green	
HR	HUMAN RESOURCES	Lt. Blue	
IT	INFORMATION TECHNOLOGY	Black	
LEG	LEGAL	Orange	
MS	MARKETING & SALES	Red	
REF	REFERENCE	White	
RD	RESEARCH / DEVELOPMENT	Brown	
SRV	SERVICE	Pink	

alpha or numeric labels, if they will improve filing and access time. Leave enough room on tabs to add more labels later.

Use caution when designing your colored-labeling system. Adding too many labels will slow the folder creation process, while too few labels will increase filing and retrieval time.

Many variations of colored labels are available. When used appropriately, colored labels can solve many filing problems. Color is used on signal labels and name labels.

Signal Labels　Preprinted signal labels are available in different sizes and colors. Each manufacturer has its own unique color scheme; consequently, once you settle on a particular brand, you are well advised not to change brands. Signal labels may be used to indicate the following types of information:

- *Alphabetic.* Colors and/or colored patterns assigned to each letter, A through Z.
- *Numeric.* Colors and/or colored patterns assigned to each number, 0 through 9.
- *Year.* Colors assigned to the last two digits of each year.
- *Month.* Colors assigned to the first three characters of each month, January through December.
- *Solid-color bars.* Colored labels in a variety of sizes and colors that can be color-coded to any folder information such as category (subject) or department.

Some manufactures also produce color-coded labels for application to top-tab folders. Due to label orientation, these labels are not interchangeable with side-tab folders, see Figure 8.8. These labels provide excellent filing aids for small filing systems.

Name Labels　Name labels are dual-purpose labels, with color identifiers as well as space for typing folder information. The downside to using these labels is the constant swapping of label stock in and out of the printer. If you are printing several labels, you may have to load and unload several different sheets of labels.

- *Color-stripe name labels.* Each label has a color stripe on the top edge. The colors can code any information such as category or department.
- *Solid-color name labels.* A full-color name label is usually available in pastels or vibrant colors. Colors can code any information such as category or department.

Figure 8.7

**Colored Side- and Top-
Tab Labels**

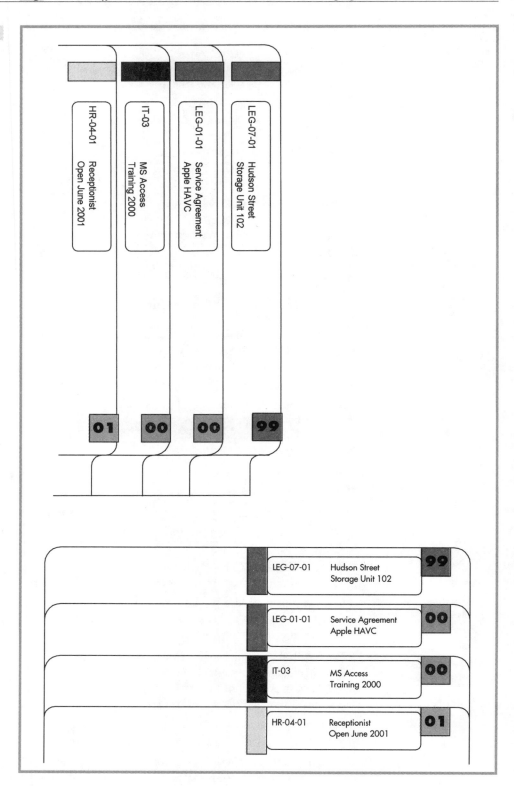

Figure 8.8

Signal and Name Labels

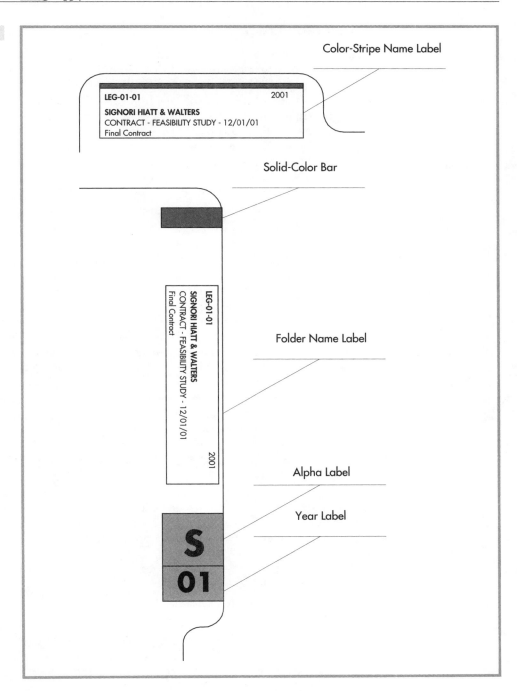

Color-Stripe Name Label

LEG-01-01   2001

SIGNORI HIATT & WALTERS
CONTRACT - FEASIBILITY STUDY - 12/01/01
Final Contract

Solid-Color Bar

LEG-01-01
SIGNORI HIATT & WALTERS
CONTRACT - FEASIBILITY STUDY - 12/01/01
Final Contract   2001

Folder Name Label

Alpha Label

Year Label

S

01

The amount of color used in your filing system will depend on the volume of folders in the system. You will need to maintain a delicate balance between asset and burden. If you have a large filing system and specific personnel to manage the system, many colored labels can be a true filing asset. On the other hand, too much color can turn your filing system into a "fruit salad" and/or create an extra burden for the staff who must apply all the labels.

Colored Folders

In the same fashion that colored labels are used as filing aids, colored folders can also be used to improve filing and finding records and information. Folders are manufactured in many different colors and, like colored labels, folder colors can be coded to denote any information. For example, a different color of folder may be used for all folders filed under a specific category or subject heading. When the color changes, the category also changes. Colored folders are available in both top-tab and side-tab versions and can be used in combination with colored labels.

Colored folders are used to tag or signal special handling for the folder contents. For example, a red folder can signal confidential documents, such as personnel records, that must not be left unattended. An orange folder may contain original documents, such as a signed agreement, that must be returned to the file vault at the end of the day.

Records Management Databases

Database software designed for active filing systems may be used to index and track active folders in an office filing system.

Records management databases can be utilized to expedite the management process of file folders. Database software designed for active filing systems may be used to index and track active folders in an office filing system. The database maintains a comprehensive index of all file folders. Most programs identify each folder by file category, folder title, storage location, department, keywords, and many other fields. These programs may be used to print folder labels and a variety of reports such as activity reports on which folders are used more often, and so on.

Not all database packages are created equal. Some will provide life-cycle management of the folders. These programs support your records retention schedule, and they can calculate transfer dates from active to inactive storage and due-for-destruction dates. Some programs may maintain the Vital Records Master List, with the records and locations identified.

Most records management database programs have separate packages for desktop PCs and networks. Generally, the more robust the program, the more expensive the product. Most records management software companies provide a trial period during which you may download a sample of the software from the Internet for testing on your office computer. Look for functionality and ease of data entry. Note whether the program will support your categories and coding system. Find out if the label design can be customized for your filing system. The overall costs should be a consideration, but not the primary consideration. Consider the qualitative factors such as the vendor's reputation, history, and references.

ARMA International's Marketplace, accessible at www.arma.org, is a good place to begin your search for records management software. To find a vendor in your area, check your *Yellow Pages'* index for *filing equipment systems and supplies.*

Notes

1. Jim Coulson, CRM, FAI, "Our Professional Responsibility," *Records Management Quarterly* 32, no. 4 (October 1998): 8.
2. Abigail J. Sellen and Richard H. R. Harper, *The Myth of the Paperless Office* (Cambridge, MA: MIT Press, 2002), 11.
3. Mary F. Robek, CRM, Gerald F. Brown, CRM, and David O. Stephens, CRM, CMC, FAI, *Information and Records Management* (New York: Glencoe/McGraw-Hill, 1996), 5.
4. Ibid., *The Myth of the Paperless Office*, 16.
5. Betty R. Ricks, CRM, Ann J. Swafford, and Kay F. Gow, *Information and Image Management: A Records System Approach* (Cincinnati, OH: South-Western Publishing Co., 1992, out of print), 11.
6. Ibid., *The Myth of the Paperless Office*, 29.

Chapter 9

Making the Change to a New Filing System

Before you do anything with your filing system, you must develop a plan. Converting your current system into an organized, efficient system is an enormous undertaking. If it isn't broken into easy tasks, the project can overwhelm you. The plan is based on the entire conversion process, which is broken into processes or tasks, with each task contributing to the whole. If you try to tackle too much, you may be setting yourself up for failure. You need to convert both paper and electronic records, not just paper.

Paper Records

As discussed in Chapters 3 and 4, you need to know what records are in your system, where they are located, and how long you need to keep them. This information is also helpful when converting from your current system to another filing arrangement or to a new, more efficient filing system. The flow chart shown in Figure 9.1 will guide you through the steps of the conversion process.

Step One – Inventory

The first step is the most critical one. Before you do anything, you must first know what records you have. Chapter 3 explains the inventory process. The information you gather here leads to the development of your retention schedule and your filing system.

Do not look at the office inventory as one big project. Instead, think small. Sketch the floor plan of the office and number all storage locations. Then move methodically through these locations, *one at a time*. Start in one location, jot down your notes on the different types of records categories stored, then move to the next location. Don't forget to inventory the electronic records.

Remember that this process is not an indexing process. In other words, you are not identifying every record or folder; you are simply gathering information on the types of records categories in each location. Use the inventory form in Appendix 2. For example, you will have files pertaining to bank statements, canceled checks, and paid invoices. Instead of identifying every folder, jot down information on the category such as how it is filed, where it is stored, approximate date ranges, and who uses the records.

> Do not look at the office inventory as one big project.

Figure 9.1
**File Conversion Plan
Flow Chart**

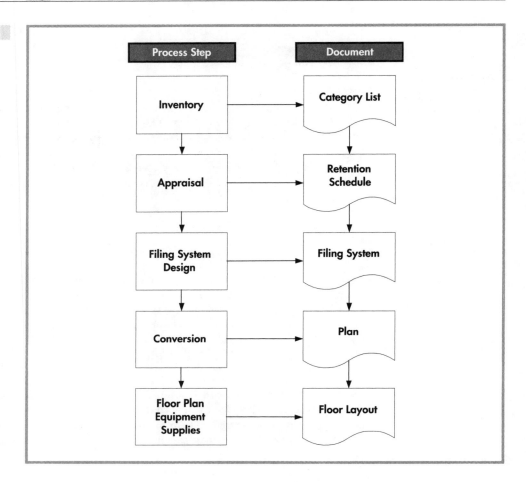

Resist the urge to begin sorting and discarding during this process. You will have plenty of time to do this work later. You can keep a trash can handy for the obvious discards such as outdated vendor brochures and catalogs, junk mail, notices on past events, etc. Do not discard or delete any records pertaining to business activities or business transactions at this time, unless you are certain they are duplicate copies.

You may use this step as an audit of your current records practices. As you move through the locations, make note of the following items:

1. Filing system problems
2. Overstuffed file cabinets
3. Excessive amount of duplicate records
4. Records in locations inconvenient for users

Step Two – Records Retention Schedule

The retention schedule establishes which records should be retained and for how long. The inventory list you created in Step One provides the basis for this schedule. Chapter 4 explains in detail how to prepare a retention schedule.

Sort the data on the inventory list into major groups, i.e., accounting, finance, legal, marketing, etc., then into the subgroups such as accounts payable, banking, marketing plan, and so on.

Customize your retention schedule to fit your needs. Compare your inventory list to the suggested Model Retention Schedule provided in Appendix 5. To meet the specific needs of *your* office, if the retention period is based solely on operational needs, you may adjust these periods. The only restriction is if a legal retention period is required. You *cannot* shorten the retention time to less than the legal requirements. For example, federal law requires that businesses retain payroll records for three years. To meet this requirement, you *must keep* these records for at least three years. Although you cannot destroy these records before three years, you may opt for, if you chose, a more conservative period and add another year to the retention period. If a question arises, a review of the federal and state statutes is recommended.

> Customize your retention schedule to fit your needs.

Step Three – Filing System Design

First, a series of choices must be made regarding the filing system. These choices include:

- Which file categories to use
- What type of coding system is most effective
- How folders will be arranged

The choices are interrelated and need to be considered together when planning the filing system. These choices are discussed in more detail in Chapter 6.

Briefly, a *file category* is a group of related files, such as accounts payable, payroll, and personnel files, stored and accessed as a collection. Each group reflects the way in which the business operates, whether operations are based on functions, activities, subject matter, or geographic locations.

Remember to keep the file categories simple. The number of categories and subcategories will depend on the volume of records. In a very small office, fewer categories are easier to manage.

Coding systems are closely interrelated to file categories. The categories should be reflected in the coding system, with categories identified by an alphabetic prefix. Again, whichever system is selected, it should be simple.

Folder arrangement is the process of putting like things together. In records management, file arrangement involves applying a filing method whereby records are stored in a systematic and consistent way in order to make retrieval quick and easy. Folders may be arranged in alphabetic, chronologic, geographic, numeric, or subject order.

Location   Where you locate the records storage units depends on who uses the records and how frequently they are accessed. Records are typically located in one of the following locations:

- *In a desk drawer.* Desk drawers are reserved for documents accessed on a daily basis, as well as for highly confidential records.
- *In a cabinet or on a shelf within an arm's reach of the primary user.* These locations should be reserved for records accessed daily or weekly by a single user.
- *In central files.* Files not used on a regular basis or files accessed by multiple users should be stored in a central file room or department.

Documenting Your Filing System Design   Once you have decided on your filing system, create a simple list that authenticates your design. A sample file arrangement list is shown in

Figure 9.2. This document isn't "etched in stone." You will be revising and adjusting the system as the conversion progresses.

Step Four – Conversion

Pull out the original floor plan used during the inventory process and follow the same path. Depending on the volume of files, the conversion may take a couple of hours to several days. Have plenty of trash bags, a paper shredder, and several records storage boxes available. You also will need office supplies such as folders, removable labels, and colored labels.

The workflow of the conversion is charted in Figure 9.3. Start where the active records are located. Do one location at a time. A location is one file cabinet, one shelving unit, a desktop, a credenza, or a box. It might also be a collection of folders on top of a desk, on the floor, or in a closet. Refer to the conversion flow chart as you read the following steps in the process.

- **Assign a Category.** Pull a folder or, in some cases, a document, out of a location. Glance through the material and assign it to the most logical category.
- **Decisions.** Once the folder is assigned to a category, making decisions about it is easier. Ask the following questions:

  1. **Keep?** Check the records against the approved retention schedule. If the date range of the materials is within the office retention period, then keep it for conversion.

     You may be surprised to know that 30 to 40 percent of the records in your files are obsolete. Have a paper shredder handy to shred those obsolete documents that contain confidential or privileged financial, employee, or client information. Some of these obsolete documents may include:

Figure 9.2

Sample File Arrangement List

Code	Category	Arrangement	Location
	My Filing System		
ACC	ACCOUNTING		
ACC-01	ACCOUNTS PAYABLE		
ACC-01-01	Invoices	By year, alphabetic by vendor name	CF - unit 1
ACC-01-02	Expense Accounts	By year, alphabetic by employee name	CF - unit 1
ACC-01-03	Reports	By year, by month	CF - unit 1
ACC-02	ACCOUNTS RECEIVABLE		
ACC-02-01	Billing / Invoices	By year, alphabetic by name	CF - unit 3
ACC-02-02	Reports	By year, by month	CF - unit 3
ACC-02-03	Collections	By year, alphabetic by name	CF - unit 1
ACC-07	TAX COMPLIANCE		
ACC-07-01	Income Tax Returns	By year	CF - unit 5
ACC-07-02	Self-Employment Tax Returns	By year, by quarter	CF - unit 5
ADM	ADMINISTRATION		
ADM-01	CALENDARS / SCHEDULES	By year	Desk
ADM-02	MEETINGS / REPORTS	By year, by month, alpha by name	CF - unit 2
ADM-03	MEMBERSHIPS	Alpha by name	CF - unit 2

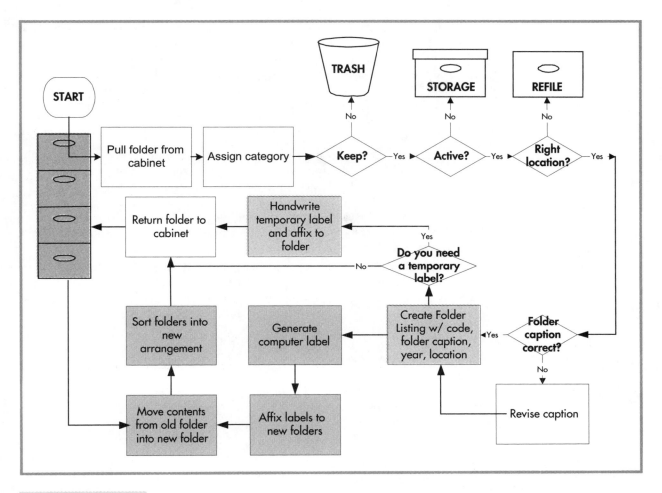

Figure 9.3
Conversion Workflow

- **Outdated business records.** Toss records for which the date ranges for all materials within a folder are past the retention period.
- **Duplicates.** Unless the records are needed for distribution, retain only one copy and toss the rest.
- **Drafts.** Retain the final version and toss the rest.
- **Outdated catalogs, brochures, flyers, solicitations, magazines, journals.** Toss.
- **Outdated forms and stationery.** Retain one or two copies in a history file and toss the rest.

2. **Active?** Check the records against the approved retention schedule. If the date ranges of the materials are within the storage period, these records are considered inactive. Inactive records are records that you must retain for legal, fiscal, or operational purposes, but you rarely reference them. For now, box the records and set them aside. After the conversion of active records is complete, you can prepare them for inactive storage.

3. **Right location?** Is the record out of place? The records should be grouped by subject or topic. If a record seems out of place, simply set it aside in a "refile" or a "to be filed elsewhere" stack. Then, when you are finished with the location, you can sort and refile these documents.

4. **Folder caption correct?** Does the folder caption make sense? Does it accurately match the folder contents? Does the caption "speak to you?" If not, choose a folder caption that reflects how you will retrieve the materials. Keep the caption simple and direct. For example, you may attend a seminar with a catchy title, such as: *"Do They Stay Because They Like You or Because They Can't Leave?"* Although this title is interesting, it may not be an easy title to remember. Filing a folder under "Customer Service" is more clear-cut and relevant.

- **Create a Folder Listing.** Add folders to a comprehensive folder listing. At minimum, the list should include location, category code, folder title, and inclusive date ranges (if applicable). You can build this listing in your spreadsheet software, custom design it with database software, or install a commercial records management database package. A spreadsheet folder listing is shown in Figure 9.4. The database program you select will depend on your technical expertise and your budget. A records management database (discussed in Chapter 8) gives you much more control over your files; however, if your file volume is small, a spreadsheet is adequate.

- **Label the Folders.** Today's printers are efficient at printing large batches of labels. First, write the label information on a temporary label, and then later, batch-enter all data into a computer for printing permanent labels.

Figure 9.4

Spreadsheet Folder List

Code	Folder Caption	Date Range	Location
FIN-09	Insurance Overview 2001 January	2001	CF- U1
FIN-09	Independent Contractor Certificate of Insurance	Current	CF- U1
FIN-09	General Package - policy 1999	1999	CF- U1
FIN-09	General Package - policy 2000	2000	CF- U1
FIN-09	General Package - policy 2001	2001	CF- U1
FIN-09	Automobile Identification	Current	CF- U1
FIN-09	Insurance Carrier Selection 2000 June	2000	CF- U1
LEG-01-01	Contractor Agreement Baldrica, Alice 2001 April	2000 - current	CF- U1
LEG-01-01	Contractor Agreement Kembel, Randall 1999 November	1999	CF- U1
LEG-01-01	Nondisclosure Agreement Henry Harris and Assoc. 2001 July	2001- current	CF- U1
LEG-07-03	Building Lease - 1777 35th Street	1999	CF- U1
LEG-07-03	Building Lease - 1990-B Walnut Street	2001	CF- U1

1. **Temporary labels.** Handprint the label data onto a removable label affixed to the folder. Other options are to use yellow sticky notes or, if the folder is to be completely replaced, write the label data directly onto the folder. Use yellow sticky notes with caution, however, as they may fall off a folder or peel off onto another folder. Affix the temporary label to the old folder and return the folder to the original file location.

2. **Permanent labels.** Permanent labels can be generated from your word processing or spreadsheet software, by using commercial label-making software, or from your records management database software. Labels may be purchased from your filing supply vendor in almost any shape, size, and color. For ease and efficiency, settle on one standard size and color of label. More than one label style will mean swapping label stock in and out of the printer, which takes too much time and energy.

3. **Label format.** Information on a label not only identifies the contents of a folder, but it is essential in filing and retrieving a folder. How information is placed onto a label must correspond with the folder arrangement. For example, the sample label in Figure 9.5 identifies the sort order: code, agreement type, contractor, date. In Figure 9.6, the sort order is identified as code, agreement type, date, contractor. How records are filed depends on how they are accessed. Use consistent formatting. Begin keying label information the same distance from the top edge and left side on each label. Use the same tab setting or the same number of spaces between sections of information, if they are used.

   In Sample 1, the contractor agreements are accessed by contractor name. In Sample 2, the contractor agreements are first accessed by the year the contractor was signed, then by name.

- **Affix New Labels to New Folders.** Use new folders in your newly organized filing system. If you are changing from drawer cabinets to shelves, use side-tab folders instead of trying to make the old drawer folders work. Top-tab folders in a shelf file reduce storage and retrieval efficiency. The files will look sloppy as well. Place labels consistently on all folders.

- **Move Folder Contents.** Once new folders are labeled and ready for use, remove the original folders and place their contents into the new folders. If some folders are too full, consider dividing the contents into two separate folders—label one folder *Vol. 1* and the second *Vol.*

Figure 9.5

File Folder Label – Sample 1

```
LEG-01-01   CONTRACTOR AGREEMENT
            BALDRICA, ALICE
            2001
```

Figure 9.6

File Folder Label – Sample 2

```
LEG-01-01   CONTRACTOR AGREEMENT
            2001
            BALDRICA, ALICE
```

2, or label the inclusive dates. Or you can separate the contents into folders labeled *Correspondence, Notes, Reports*, etc.

- **Sort Folders into the New Arrangement.** Finally, you are ready to implement your new filing system. Follow the folder order in the *Filing System Design* that you established in Step Three.

Step Five – Floor Plan

At the conclusion of the folder conversion, you will know the exact volume of your filing system, and you can more easily make decisions about your filing space. Folders you just converted probably will not stay in their original locations. If you decide to move any of them at a later date, follow the folder location instructions from your *Filing System Design* plan. Put your new floor plan (space map), as discussed in Chapter 7, into practice. Make adjustments, where necessary.

Electronic Records

Electronic records are organized and managed in much the same way as paper records. Electronic documents are records just as paper documents are records. The retention schedule you developed for paper records is applied in exactly the same fashion to electronic records. The filing system you developed for paper records also works for electronic records.

As you begin to convert your electronic records to a new system, examine electronic documents as you would a paper file:

> Electronic documents are records just as paper documents are records.

- **Assign a File Category.** Assign logical categories. They will probably be the same categories you use for paper records.
- **Decisions:**
  1. **Official copy?** Which record is the official copy? The electronic record or the paper record? The **official record** is the copy the business retains to meet the legal, fiscal, and/or operational retention requirements. Most of us keep both the paper and electronic forms of a record for convenience, because either the electronic copies are easier to locate, or they may be useful as document templates or boilerplates. If the electronic copy is only a working copy of the document, then the official copy is the paper copy. Secondary copies may be kept; however, they may not be retained any longer than specified in the retention schedule.
  2. **Keep?** Check documents against the approved retention schedule.
     - **Outdated documents.** Delete documents on which the date is past the retention period.
     - **Duplicates.** Retain only one copy and delete the others.
     - **Drafts.** Retain the final version and delete the others.
  3. **Active?** Check the document against the approved retention schedule. If the date of the document is within the date ranges of the inactive storage period, then these records are considered inactive. Inactive records are records that you must retain for legal, fiscal, or operational purposes, but you rarely reference them. Tag the records for the following:

> Inactive records are records that you must retain for legal, fiscal, or operational purposes, but you rarely reference them.

     - Migration to another media such as CD-ROM, digital audio tape (DAT) tape, floppy disk, Zip disk, etc., or
     - Compression and storage in a segregated space on your network or hard drive.

4. **Document title / label correct?** Does the title or label make sense? Does it accurately match the document contents? Does the title "speak to you?" If not, choose a label that reflects how you will retrieve the information. Keep the label simple and direct.

- **Identification.** Identify each document by its category code. Most document database programs have file identification summary fields. Summary fields are details about a file that help identify it. For each document, you can set the category code as a file property. For example, you can add the category LEG-01-01 to all your agreement files and then search for all files with that category.

- **Code location.** Place the category code in a visible location on each document, such as in the footer, so that it prints on every page or on the last line of the document.

Chapter 10

The Follow-Through— Maintenance Tips

To keep your records in good order, you must continue to manage them. Ongoing records management procedures consist of setting up maintenance routines to make sure that once organized, the records stay organized.

As much as you would like, you cannot set up a filing system and expect it to stay organized without some effort. The system requires regular routines to keep it organized. Otherwise, vast quantities of inactive paper-based records will clog expensive office space, which makes retrieving essential information virtually impossible.

Active Records Maintenance

Because active records are used to generate business or to follow up on active business transactions, they need to be well organized and accessible.

Active records, as discussed in Chapter 1, are those records most frequently referred to in the daily operations of your business. Because active records are used to generate business or to follow up on active business transactions, they need to be well organized and accessible.

Document Decisions

Don't allow documents to pile up. Every document that comes across your desk requires an immediate action of some type. Possible decisions include:

1. **Act on it now.** Immediately follow through on the requested action, or

2. **Hold it for later.** If the document is on a temporary hold, store it in a pending file folder. Some examples of hold actions include:

   - *Hold for Action.* If you're unable to answer a letter or respond to a request on the day received, file it in an action folder. Set a weekly appointment to deal with this file.

   - *Hold for Activity.* If the document needs to be held for handling on a future date, file it in a tickler file. An expanding folder with pockets for each day of the month may be used as a tickler folder for daily activities. For example, if you are holding tickets for a trade show that you plan to attend, file the tickets in a pocket corresponding to the day of the trade show. Every day, check the "today" pocket.

   - *Hold for Payment.* You may have a regular monthly or weekly payment routine for paying bills or for batch-entering debit items into your electronic ledger. Invoices or bills may be held in a payment folder until then.

- *Hold for Reading.* When you receive a report, meeting minutes or a magazine you want to read but can't deal with immediately, place it into a reading file. Take the reading file with you in your briefcase to make the most of any downtime at any location.

3. **Forward.** If someone else would benefit more from the document, forward it to that person or group.

4. **Toss.** Is the document out-of-date, obsolete, redundant, unnecessary, irrelevant, or substandard? If it is, toss it. Do not allow junk mail and unsolicited advertising material to inundate your work area. If any document has no current relevance to you or to your clients, toss it. Keep a wastebasket nearby while opening your mail.

5. **File.** If action has already been taken, file the document.

Filing Tips

File regularly. Set aside time daily or at least weekly to keep the paper under control. Documents filed promptly will be available when needed.

Determining What to File   In the course of every day, a variety of documents will be received or sent from your offices. Consequently, you must decide how to handle originals, copies, drafts, and various forms.

- **Correspondence** is the most common method of conducting business. For filing purposes, correspondence may be separated into transitory or substantive documents. **Transitory records** have short-term value and **substantive records** have long-term value. Transitory correspondence includes routine requests, form letters, cover letters, FYI memos, etc. The retention period for transitory records is limited to the interval period required for completion of the action covered by the communication.

  Substantive correspondence contains business transaction information such as purchasing instructions or letters of agreement. Substantive correspondence documents are filed within a subject category that matches its contents and therefore its retention period. For example, substantive correspondence pertaining to a particular project should be filed with the documents for that project such as CR-02. Transitory correspondence is usually filed in a general correspondence file such as ADM-01.

- **Drafts** should be tossed after newer versions or the final version supersedes them.

- **Reminders, worksheets, extra copies, telephone messages, sticky notes, etc.,** should not be filed unless they contain substantive information.

Preparing Documents for Filing
- Remove temporary fasteners such as rubber bands, paper clips, and binder clips.
- Verify that the document is complete by accounting for all pages, enclosures, and attachments.
- Verify that either parts or entire documents are not attached or clipped to the document.
- Wherever possible, file the original document and not a photocopy. Similarly, the original document and not a faxed document should be filed. If you have a thermal copy of a fax, photocopy the fax, and file the photocopy.

Assigning Documents to a Subject Category
- Skim the contents of a document to determine the file category.
- Write the category code in the top right corner of each document.

- Presort documents into category code order before filing.

Placing Documents into File Folders
- Match the category code on each document with the code on the folder label before filing it in the folder.
- File documents in chronologic order with the most recently dated document on top.

Tips for Keeping Files in Good Condition

- Put a label on each file drawer and shelf that adequately identifies the contents. For example, see Figure 10.1.
- Use consistent formatting on labels. (See Chapter 8.)
- Allow two to three inches of extra space in each drawer or shelf to permit sufficient working space.
- Do not fill a folder beyond its capacity: Three-fourths of an inch of materials is the maximum capacity of a standard manila folder. Score the folder (i.e., fold along the folder's prescored creases) to accommodate its contents.
- If the contents of a folder grow beyond the capacity of the folder, divide the contents into more than one folder. Label captions on the new folders should specify the contents, as shown in Figure 10.2.
- Keep records completely within folders to avoid damaging the contents and to keep the folder label visible.
- Develop a fixed label layout so that similar information always appears in the same location on each label. See Figure 10.3.
- Select a fixed location for each folder label. See Figure 10.4.

Figure 10.1

Drawer Labels

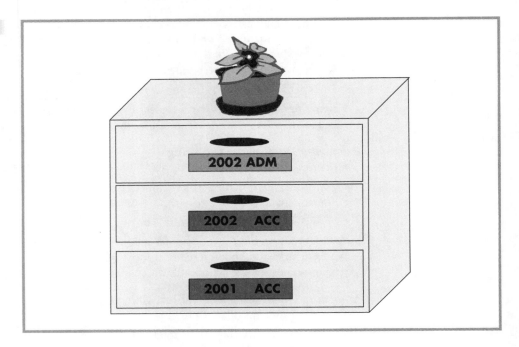

Figure 10.2

Divide Overflowing Folders

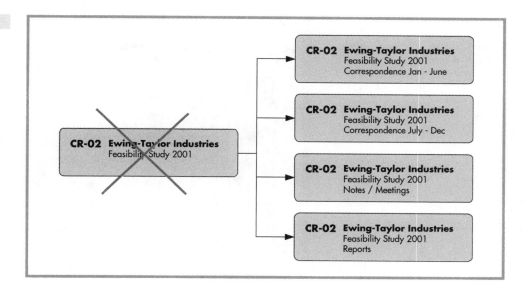

Figure 10.3

Inconsistent vs. Consistent Label Captions

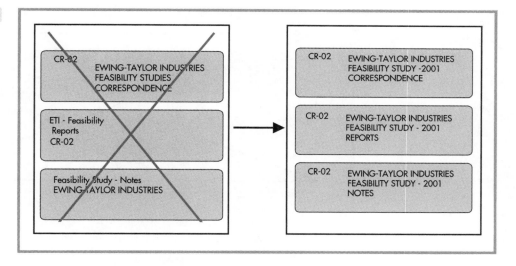

- Do not randomly stagger folder tabs within a drawer or shelf. Instead, align folder tabs to match your category-coding scheme. The eye sees in straight lines, and filing is much more efficient if the tabs follow a straight line in a drawer or on a shelf. See Figure 10.5.

Desktop Organization

- To save retrieval time, the filing cabinet containing the records you use most frequently should be within an arm's reach of your desk.

- Do not leave folders on your desk. Refile folders as soon as possible. Use an out card or guide to speed refiling.

- Don't create miscellaneous folders. Trying to remember what is filed in miscellaneous folders is difficult, and they are an easy place to lose or misplace documents.

Figure 10.4

**Inconsistent vs.
Consistent Label
Placement**

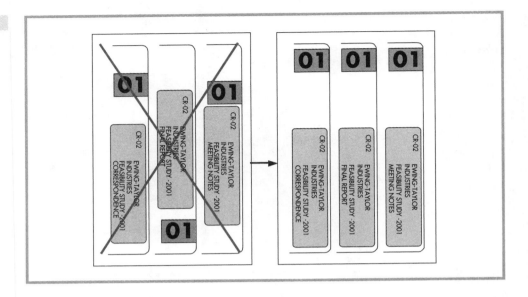

Figure 10.5

**Staggered vs. Straight-
Line Folder Tabs**

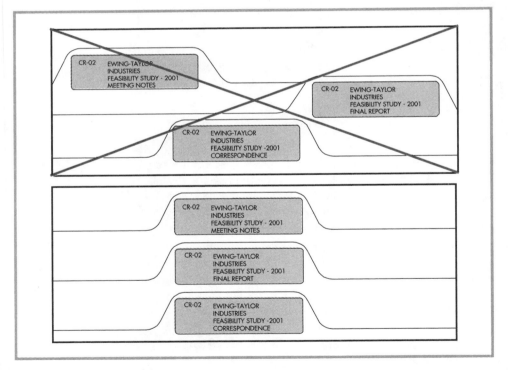

Statistics show that up to
three percent of all documents are misfiled or misplaced, and over seven
percent are just plain lost.

Tips for Locating a Misfile

Everyone at one time or another has lost a document or a file. Statistics show that up to three
percent of all documents are misfiled or misplaced, and over seven percent are just plain lost.[1]
Following good filing procedures should greatly reduce misfiles. If you do misplace a file,
before you panic, logically think through where the document may have been misplaced:

- Check all documents in the folder to see if the missing document was incorrectly positioned in the folder.
- Check in folders directly in front, behind, and under the proper folder. The document may have been incorrectly filed in an adjacent folder.
- Check between folders. When filing, the document may have slipped between folders instead of into a folder.
- Check variations on spelling and synonyms.
- Check related categories to see if the document was filed under the wrong category.
- Check "to be filed" trays and piles.
- Check with coworkers. Someone else may have it.
- Check wastebaskets and recycle bins. It may have been tossed by mistake.

Electronic Records Maintenance

Electronic records are documents stored on electronic storage media that can be readily accessed or changed. Some electronic records continue to be maintained, transmitted, and retrieved in electronic format. They may be printed for distribution, but the official record is maintained as an electronic record. Remember that an official record is a document maintained by the business as evidence of an activity.

You will also keep nonofficial records, also known as *nonrecords*, in electronic format. **Nonrecords** are items that are not usually included within the scope of official records, e.g., convenience file, day file, reference materials, drafts, etc. They are documents not required to be retained and therefore do not appear on a records retention schedule. They may be drafts or copies of official records and informational or reference documents.

Many businesses keep electronic templates or boilerplates as records. These records are usually copies of documents, such as contracts, correspondence, reports, etc., stored in electronic format and used to create new documents. For example, you may have a boilerplate contract that you routinely print for new clients.

Managing Electronic Records

All federal agencies recognize electronic records as official records.

- Official records maintained in electronic format should be stored in read-only format. Once a document is final, it should not be changed.
- When official records become inactive, they should be transferred to a separate area on the hard drive or to an off-line storage medium such as optical disk, CD-ROM, magnetic disk, or magnetic tape. Continue to monitor these records to keep them in compliance with your retention schedule.
- All federal agencies recognize electronic records as official records. For example, the Internal Revenue Service (IRS) has provisions (Rev. Proc. 97-22) for storing records on electronic media such as optical disk, CD-ROM, and computer-output to laser disk (COLD).
- To prevent transitory documents and nonrecords from cluttering hard drives, you need to periodically review them and destroy those you have not accessed in over a year.

Quick Tip for Your Legal or Tax Advisor: IRS Rev. Proc. 97-22

Summary: Provides guidance to those institutions that maintain electronic records utilizing scanning or imaging of hard copies or that transfer electronic records to an electronic storage media.

The system must:
- Be accurate and reliable; inspected periodically; highly legible; indexed;
- Provide an audit trail from original entry to the tax return;
- Provide resources for retrieving information at the time of an IRS exam, audit, or evaluation.

- Boilerplate records should be kept in a separate file from official records. A standard boilerplate should be stripped of any information that may confuse it with the official record. For example, a boilerplate contract should not be an exact duplicate of an official contract.

Labeling and Identifying Off-Line Media

Official records retained off-line on optical disk, CD-ROM, magnetic disk, and magnetic tape, etc., must be appropriately identified and labeled. External labels should include:

- Name or title captions of contents
- Inclusive dates
- File category
- Destruction date
- Software application and version (e.g., MS Word 2000, Peachtree 2002)
- Operating system and version, if more than one is used (Window 98, Windows XP, Mac)

Tips for Managing E-mail Records

- **Decisions:** E-mail often contains important information that you will want to keep. Use the following criteria for determining what e-mail to keep.
  1. Is it a duplicate? If 25 other people received it, chances are you don't need it. Delete.
  2. Did you request this information? If it was unsolicited, why keep it? Delete.
  3. Would someone else benefit more from this information? If yes, forward and delete.
  4. Does this information help with my business objectives? If not, delete.
  5. Is the information available elsewhere? If yes, delete.
  6. What is the worst that could happen if this information were deleted?
- **Organize:**
  1. Create folders to organize the information into specific subject groups.
  2. Keep the inbox as clean as possible. When an e-mail message is received, read, file, forward, move, and/or delete the message.
- **Identify:**
  1. Identify the business documents. If the information is valuable, transfer the document (the e-mail message and/or the e-mail attachment) out of the e-mail directory to a more meaningful directory and assign it to a category.
  2. For longer-term retention of e-mail documents, print them, and store in folders.

Vital Records Maintenance

Establish regular routines to review your Vital Records Protection Plan. (See Chapter 5 for more information on vital records.) These routines will provide peace of mind that you know where your vital records are stored and what to do in a time of crisis. Remember that the welfare of your business may depend on your vital records.

Remember that the welfare of your business may depend on your vital records.

Once a Month

- Check the validity of your computer backups to make certain your data can be restored from the back-up media.

Every Six Months

- Review the Vital Records Master List for additions, substitutions, and deletions, and update as appropriate. (See Chapter 5.)

- Copy the new list for every team member.

Once a Year

- Emergency Contacts:
    1. Verify that the information on the recovery team is up-to-date.
    2. Verify that your contact lists of consequence management specialists, such as maintenance contractors, data recovery companies, salvage and recovery companies, are up-to-date.
- Test the System:
    1. Practice your disaster procedures to verify that the procedures are complete, efficient, and successful.

Retention Maintenance

The routine application of your records retention schedule will decrease the amount of paper in your office, increase the amount of available space, and improve staff efficiency.

Establish regular routines for monitoring records retention. The routine application of your records retention schedule will decrease the amount of paper in your office, increase the amount of available space, and improve staff efficiency. You want to:

- Reduce the number of files in an office.
- Improve retrieval time, as fewer files need to be searched.
- Keep the business in compliance with your records retention schedules.

Tips for Year-End Cleanup Days

During December or January (or the months following the end of your fiscal year), hold *Year-End Cleanup Days* to encourage staff to retire records, as specified in the retention schedule.

Paper Records Your retention schedule should state how long records are stored in the active / office area and how long records are stored in the inactive / storage area.

- Move inactive records out of the active file area. See the "Packing Boxes for Storage" section later in this chapter for tips on how to pack inactive records for storage.
- Properly dispose of records that have met their retention requirements, according to the records retention schedule. The method of destruction will depend upon the nature of the materials:
    - *Shred* confidential, fiscal, and client records. Shred anything with social security numbers, bank account numbers, credit card numbers, and other personal information.
    - *Toss or recycle* nonconfidential and routine records.
- Prepare a new set of annual file folders for the new calendar (fiscal) year. Annual file folders are folders that contain one year's worth of records such as accounting, financial, and administrative records.

Personal Work Space

- Empty and reorganize your desk. Weed through all papers that have been collecting and trash anything that is expired or not vital to your existence. Move the rest to a Reading or Action folder or file it.
- Toss outdated reading materials such as journals and magazines that are older than six months. If you find an article you would like to read, rip it out, and place it into your Reading folder.
- Toss catalogs and sales brochures in which you have no interest.
- Toss old business cards and update your contact management database.

Electronic Records
- Move inactive records out of the active area to either:
  - A separate area on the hard drive; or
  - An off-line storage medium such as optical disk, CD-ROM, magnetic disk, or magnetic tape.
- Delete official records that have met their retention requirements, per the records retention schedule.
- Delete nonofficial and informational records that have not been accessed in the last year.
- Review all e-mails over six months old. Identify the business documents. If the information is valuable, transfer the document out of the e-mail directory to a more meaningful directory and assign it to a category. Delete nonofficial and informational e-mails that are over six months old. Print and file e-mails for long-term retention.

Tips for Every Other Year

- Review your records retention schedule to determine whether all records are identified and whether the retention periods are still meeting your operational needs.
- Update the retention schedule as necessary.

Inactive Paper Records

> Because of their low reference rate, inactive records should be physically separated from active records.

Inactive records are rarely accessed, maybe once a month or less, but they are not yet due for destruction. Because of their low reference rate, inactive records should be physically separated from active records.

Where you store inactive records depends on the space and filing equipment available. If space is not an issue and you have extra file cabinets or shelves that can be set up in a secure, protected, out-of-the-way place, then, by all means, use this space for inactive records storage.

Not all offices are fortunate enough to have much available filing space. Most offices must make use of the limited space that is available. If space is an issue, then a high-density solution, such as storing the records in boxes, may be the answer.

Packing Boxes for Storage

The dimensions of a standard records box are 10 inches high by 12 inches wide by 15 inches deep. You can determine the number of boxes you will need by using this guide: For letter-size files, two full drawers will fill three standard boxes; for legal-size files, one full drawer will fill two standard boxes.

- For undersize materials, you must calculate the total number of linear inches of items. Pack records in the same order in which they are maintained in the active files.
- Pack boxes loosely. Records may need to be added later.
- Do not pack informational records, working copies, convenience copies, etc.
- Do not pack hanging files or loose-leaf binders. If records are in hanging files or binders, refile them into manila folders. Make sure to label the folders to identify their contents.
- Do not mix paper records with magnetic diskettes, optical disks, or magnetic tapes. Use storage equipment suited for these types of media.

Quick Tip: Hanging Files

Records managers in many large organizations have learned that refoldering items stored in hanging files is a labor-intensive task. Consequently, they will often simply remove the hanging files and their contents and place them into boxes for storage.

The cost of labor, for a large volume of files, sometimes is more than the cost of replacing the hanging folders. Be sure you analyze your costs carefully.

Do not mix paper records with magnetic diskettes, optical disks, or magnetic tapes.

- Remember! These boxed records will be stored and destroyed as a unit because they represent a records series or a category. Check the retention schedule of the records so that you do not store records with different retention periods in the same box.

- Using a permanent marker pen, write the box number on the narrow end of the box to the left of the handgrip, as shown in Figure 10.6.

Storage Solutions

Where you store inactive records depends on your access requirements. If you need very quick access, such as less than an hour, an on-site solution is needed. If a 24-hour turn-around time is acceptable, a commercial records center will do.

Commercial Records Center   A **commercial records center** stores the records of several organizations and provides services on a fee basis. It is a professionally staffed repository used to warehouse large quantities of inactive business records. Monthly fee rates for box storage are based on a per-box, per-cubic-foot, or a per-square-foot basis. Additional labor charges are added for adding, removing, accessing, and delivering boxes.

Center staff will maintain a database of your records. They can also provide reports that will include a listing of all boxes stored in the center, when they were sent to the center, how often they were accessed, when they are due for destruction, etc.

These centers are particularly appealing to businesses lacking adequate space for storing inactive records. Most commercial centers offer quick delivery of requested records. The centers offer security from human intrusion and protection from natural disasters. Additional services may include on-line access to your inactive records database, environmentally controlled areas for electronic records storage, and certified records destruction services.

Before deciding on a center, you should ask to inspect the facility and thoroughly check out the center's customer service reputation.

Before deciding on a center, you should ask to inspect the facility and thoroughly check out the center's customer service reputation.

On-Site Storage   Another option is to build a high-density storage area inside your office. Suitable locations include storage closets or vacant offices. Factors to take into account when selecting a location include security and safety, as well as protection from adverse environmental conditions and pest infestations.

You may consider storing business records in your building's basement, a miniwarehouse (self-storage), or in another unsecured location. Although these areas may be economical, they are not good records storage locations. Basements are vulnerable to ground water flooding, broken water pipes, insects, and rodents. If the area is not adequately secured, the boxes are vulnerable to vandalism, and the confidentiality of the box contents cannot be guaranteed. With miniwarehouses, your records are even more vulnerable. In addition to its lack of security and exposure to insects and rodents, you will never know what is stored in a neighboring unit. The next unit's contents could be harmless, or it could contain hazardous materials such as flammable painting supplies or gasoline.

High-Density Storage Design

The goal in setting up a storage area is to establish a high-density storage solution. A simple method is to equip it with industrial-type steel shelving, with shelves measuring 15 inches deep by 42

Figure 10.6

Storage Box Number

inches long to accommodate three standard records boxes. The height of the unit will depend upon the ceiling allowances, and, if applicable, local fire codes that state the acceptable distance from the highest point of the shelving unit to a ceiling fire sprinkler.

Within the unit, each space is assigned a unique address: a unit-space numbering system. To create an address, assign each shelving unit a number and each space within the unit a number. See Figure 10.7.

When a box is put into storage, it is assigned an address. This address is written on the box and stays with the box until the contents of the box are destroyed. Using a permanent marker pen, write the address on the narrow end of the box in an area below the handgrip, as shown in Figure 10.8.

Box Index

A finding aid serves as a directory to the inactive records. You can easily set up a finding aid, or box index, using a word processing or spreadsheet program, see Figure 10.9. The advantage of using a word processing table or a spreadsheet is that you can sort the information many different ways. You would keep the list sorted alphabetically by folder description most of the time.

Begin by defining your sort categories. Here's an example of some information you might want to track within separate fields:

- Classification code (Code)
- File description (Desc)
- Date range (Date)
- Disposition date (Disp)

Figure 10.7

Storage Shelves Containing Records Boxes

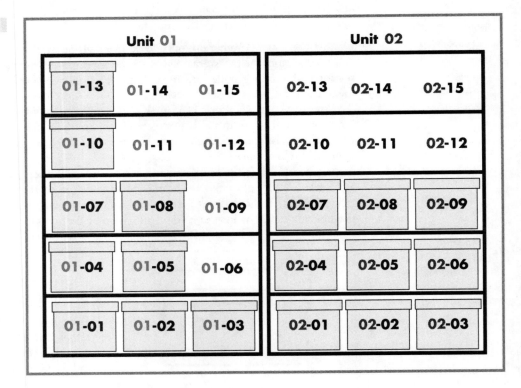

- Box number (Box#)
- Box Location (Loc)

If you use a spreadsheet or a word processing table, the first row would include the field names. Each successive row would contain information for one folder.

- Enter information for each file under the appropriate category;
- Sort files by file title (alphabetic) order for easy reference;
- Sort files by box location to identify the contents of each box;
- A hard copy in alphabetic order is useful for staff members to browse when searching for a record.

In Closing: Beyond This Book

Many businesses are stretched to the limit on time and staffing. If you do not have the time or lack the confidence to undertake a files reorganization project on your own, outside help is available. ARMA International is a professional organization serving the records and information management community. The organization sponsors many educational programs, including conferences, seminars, and workshops, on records and information management. For further study, ARMA International also publishes journals, books, and videos on records and information management, vital records, emergency management, disaster recovery, and electronic records and information. A sampling of ARMA publications is listed in Appendix 6.

ARMA International's Web site at www.arma.org contains an abundance of information on the records and information profession. You may also find a link to an ARMA International chapter site in your area so that you can contact local individuals and learn more about local resources such as seminars, workshops, and consultants.

Professional records management consulting services usually provide assistance with retention scheduling and active files management, as well as expertise in developing records management policy and procedure. These services are performed by a records management consultant, frequently with a certified records manager (CRM) certification. These individuals are available in every area of the United States. Check with a local ARMA International chapter to find a consultant in your area.

Figure 10.8

Storage Box Number and Address

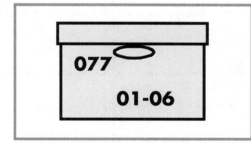

Notes

1. Abigail J. Sellen and Richard H.R Harper, *The Myth of the Paperless Office* (Cambridge, MA: MIT Press, 2002), 11.

Figure 10.9

Inactive Records in Storage

Box Index						
Code	Desc		Date	Disp	Box#	Loc
LEG-01-01	Midas Gold - Confidentiality Ag.		1999	2008	077	01-06
LEG-01-01	Midas Gold - ROW Ag.		1998	2007	052	01-04
LEG-01-01	Arrowhead Corp. - Service Ag.		1997	2005	049	02-03

Standard Records Categories

Standard categories are a series of subjects, arranged into **major** categories, and then further defined into **primary** categories, and if necessary, into **secondary** categories.

Code: Unique identifiers assigned to each category. The code is a three-part formula: AA-NN-NN. The alpha characters identify the major category grouping, the first set of numbers identify the primary category, and the second set, if applicable, identify the secondary category.

Name: The name is the identification or term used to label the category.

Description: The description explains and clarifies the inclusive subject contents of the category. The description may also include document types that belong to this category.

    The categories do <u>not</u> identify individual file folders. They are presented as a guide to assist you in defining your own categories. These categories may be edited or modified to meet your own specific coding and naming conventions. You should revise and fine-tune the category names and descriptions so that they comply with your business style.

Code	Name	Description
ACC	ACCOUNTING	Records pertaining to fiscal recordkeeping practices, records of transactions used as the basis for recording accounting entries. Includes invoices, check stubs, receipts, and similar business papers.
ACC-01	ACCOUNTS PAYABLE	Records pertaining to financial obligations, funds owed to a supplier for goods or services purchased on credit. (Also known as A/P.) Includes chart of accounts, ledgers, reports, and source documentation such as invoices and vouchers. General information.
ACC-01-01	Invoices	Includes statements and invoices from suppliers; customer refunds; license and registration fees; rental and lease payments; payments of fees or dues of memberships.
ACC-01-02	Expense Accounts	Includes accounts for business expenses that have been paid or incurred in the course of business and that are ordinary, necessary, and reasonable.
ACC-01-03	Ledger/Register	A/P ledger.
ACC-01-04	Reports	Periodic or special A/P reports.
ACC-02	ACCOUNTS RECEIVABLE	Records pertaining to funds due and payable to the business. A current asset representing money due for services performed or merchandise sold on credit. (Also known as A/R.) Includes ledgers, reports, and source documentation from commissions, customer payments, fees, and refunds. General information.

Code	Name	Description
ACC-02-01	Billing/Invoices	Records pertaining to invoicing and billing activities for services or products sold.
ACC-02-02	Reports	A/R reports.
ACC-02-03	Collections	Records related to uncollectable funds and debts sent to third-party collection.
ACC-03	CASH MANAGEMENT	Records pertaining to cash receipts and cash disbursements. Includes journals and reconciliations.
ACC-03-01	Journal	Cash management journal.
ACC-04	COST ACCOUNTING	Records pertaining to costing systems and cost determination for materials, labor, and overheads. Includes cost centers, analysis, and reports.
ACC-04-01	Cost Ledger	Cost accounting ledger.
ACC-05	GENERAL LEDGER	Records pertaining to the recording of the book of accounts, with all account transactions of the business, including its assets, liabilities, etc. Includes (automated or manual) journals, ledgers, and reports.
ACC-05-01	Journal	Accounting record in which transactions are entered; a chronologic record of all business activities.
ACC-05-02	Subledgers	Subledgers (subsidiary ledgers) of individual accounts that in total equal the balance of a control account in the General Ledger.
ACC-05-03	Supporting Documents	Documents or records that support transactions.
ACC-06	PAYROLL	Records pertaining to salary and compensation. Includes records of individual employees. General information.
ACC-06-01	Payroll/Registers	Includes employee information, salary and wages payments, payroll adjustments, benefit information, W-2 forms.
ACC-06-02	Time Sheets	Records regarding tracking of employee time for purposes of payroll, billing, or activities.
ACC-06-03	Reports	Statistical information related to payroll practices.
ACC-06-04	W-2 Forms	Employee W-2 Forms.
ACC-06-05	W-4 Forms	Employee W-4 Forms.
ACC-07	TAX COMPLIANCE	Local, state, and federal tax returns or payments, including sales, payroll, and income taxes. General information.
ACC-07-01	Income Tax Returns	Federal, state, and local income tax.
ACC-07-02	Payroll/Employment Tax Returns	Tax payments, including social security, federal withholding tax, and state withholding tax. Includes records on amounts withheld and records on tax deposits and electronic payments.
ACC-07-03	Property Tax Returns	Property tax returns.
ACC-07-04	Sales Tax Returns	Sales tax returns.
ACC-07-05	Self-Employment Tax Returns	Returns for self-employment taxes, including quarterly payment records.
ADM	ADMINISTRATION	Records pertaining to the planning, supervising, and managing of the daily activities of the business.
ADM-01	CORRESPONDENCE/GENERAL	Letters, notes, e-mails, memos pertaining to a general inquiry or response, chronologic files, etc., that are referred to shortly after received or created but have no lasting value.
ADM-02	CALENDARS/SCHEDULES	Yearly, monthly, daily calendars, appointment books, date books, schedulers, etc.
ADM-03	MEETINGS/REPORTS	Periodic and special administrative meetings and reports.
ADM-04	MEMBERSHIPS	Records pertaining to memberships in industry or professional associations or organizations. Includes membership rosters, directories, meeting information, conference or convention information.
ADM-05	EQUIPMENT/FURNITURE	Includes office furniture, equipment, computers, vehicles, and tools. Includes lease programs, purchases, etc. General information.
ADM-05-01	Inventory Lists	Records pertaining to the inventory/tracking of business owned, leased, or rented equipment and vehicles. (Does not pertain to inventory of goods held for resale.)
ADM-05-02	Maintenance	Records pertaining to maintaining business owned, leased, or rented furniture, office equipment, computers, vehicles, and tools.

Code	Name	Description
ADM-05-03	Manuals	User or operating manuals for business owned, leased, or rented furniture, office equipment, computers, vehicles, and tools.
ADM-05-04	Warranties	Records pertaining to warranties and guarantee information on currently owned equipment and products. Includes service contracts, invoices, claims, etc.
ADM-06	FACILITIES	Records pertaining to building, office, land, and property management. General information.
ADM-06-01	Building Maintenance	Records pertaining to building, office, land, and property maintenance, repair, and upkeep.
ADM-06-02	Security	Records pertaining to the protection of equipment, products, building, office, land, and employees. Includes records on access cards or keys, computer access, clearance access, policies, and procedures.
ADM-06-03	Space Planning/Plans	Records pertaining to space planning and layout. Includes building blue prints, design plans, interior decorating plans, landscaping plans, etc.
ADM-07	FORMS/SUPPLIES	Records pertaining to provision of office materials and supplies, including forms, reprographics, filing, and postal. Includes catalogs and ordering information.
ADM-08	POLICY AND PROCEDURES	Records related to policies, methods, and processes that document uniform business practices.
ADM-09	RECORDS MANAGEMENT	Records pertaining to the records management program and to records storage and retrieval. Includes file lists and off-site storage inventory lists. General information.
ADM-09-01	Manuals	Manuals pertaining to records management polices and procedures. Includes filing manuals, filing procedures, classification lists.
ADM-09-02	Retention Schedule	Records pertaining to records retention and disposition schedules. Includes official retention schedule and certificates of destruction.
ADM-10	VENDORS	Records pertaining to the products and services from outside sources. Includes reference materials on product information, price lists, catalogs, brochures, etc.
ADM-11	CONSULTANTS	Records regarding outside consulting services. Includes fee information, work history, and references.
ADM-12	CONTRACTORS/ SUBCONTRACTORS	Records pertaining to contractors or subcontractors the business works with in the regular course of business. Includes fee information, work history, and references. (Does not include financial contractors, consultants, or outside legal counsel.)
ADM-13	OFFICE FUNCTIONS	Records pertaining to business-sponsored office and employee programs. Includes newsletters, announcements, parties, and activities.
ADM-14	PRESENTATION MATERIALS	Records pertaining to outside presentations received or attended regarding professional or industry information.
ADM-15	REFERENCE	Records pertaining to library and/or reference materials collected or received regarding professional or industry information. Includes publications, bulletins, books, magazines, newsletters, journals, etc.
CR	CLIENT RELATIONS	Records pertaining to management of clients or customers regarding the sale of products and/or services.
CR-01	CLIENTS/ACCOUNTS	Records pertaining to individual customer or client accounts. Includes correspondence, proposals, commitments, follow-ups, etc.
CR-02	PROJECTS/SPECIAL PROJECTS	Records pertaining to the work product for individual customer or client projects or special projects. Includes records of all deliverables.
CR-03	COMPLAINTS	Records pertaining to customer complaints about products, services, or performance.
COR	CORPORATE	Records pertaining to corporation organization and governance.
COR-01	ARTICLES OF INCORPORATION/ BYLAWS	Records pertaining to the creation and formation of the corporation and the bylaws of the corporation.
COR-02	BOARD OF DIRECTORS	Records pertaining to formal meetings and minutes of the corporation's board of directors. General information.

Code	Name	Description
COR-02-01	Minutes/Meetings	Records pertaining to meetings of the corporate board of directors, including notices, agenda items, official meeting minutes, reports, and back-up materials.
COR-02-02	Committees/Meetings	Records pertaining to meetings of the corporate committees, including notices, agenda items, official meeting minutes, reports, and back-up materials.
COR-03	SHAREHOLDERS	Records pertaining to the corporation's shareholders. Includes records on the annual meeting, proxies, script, and back-up materials. General information.
COR-03-01	Annual Reports	Corporate annual reports.
COR-03-02	SEC Reports	Corporate SEC reports such as 10-K, 10-Q, etc.
COR-04	STOCKS	Records pertaining to the issuance of stock and stock certificates by a corporation to stockholders evidencing ownership in the corporation.
COR-04-01	Dividend Records	Records pertaining to dividend payments. Includes canceled dividend checks and receipts acknowledging payment.
FIN	FINANCE	Records pertaining to fiscal management of assets, liabilities, funds, and investments.
FIN-01	ASSETS	Records pertaining to anything owned by a business that has financial value. Includes information on when the assets were acquired and how much they cost. General information.
FIN-01-01	Fixed Assets	Records pertaining to tangible, long-lived assets acquired for use in business operations. Includes land, buildings, machinery, equipment, and furniture.
FIN-01-02	Depreciation	Records pertaining to plant or equipment (tangible fixed assets) depreciation, calculating the declining value, due to such causes as wear and tear, action of the elements, inadequacy, and obsolescence, but without loss of substance.
FIN-01-03	Inventory	Records pertaining to the amount of goods held for resale on hand at any given time. Includes Inventory control records, item perpetual inventory records. Stock plan, out-of-stock sheet.
FIN-02	AUDITS	The result of a review of records and documents to determine compliance with generally accepted accounting principles and the reliability, accuracy, and completeness of financial and administrative records and reports. General information.
FIN-02-01	Internal	Records pertaining to internal reviews, audits, or investigations of business practices.
FIN-02-02	External	Records pertaining to reviews, audits, or investigations from outside sources such as federal and state government agencies to ensure compliance with applicable statutes, regulations, policies, and prescribed procedures.
FIN-03	BANKING	Records pertaining to business transactions with any banking institution. General information.
FIN-03-01	Statements	Records pertaining to a monthly statement of account mailed by a bank to each of its customers with accounts, recording the banking transactions and current balance during a specific period.
FIN-03-02	Canceled Checks	Records that are canceled checks redeemed by a bank and returned to the account owner.
FIN-03-03	Foreign Accounts	Records pertaining to accounts with foreign banks.
FIN-03-04	Petty Cash Fund	Records pertaining to a small amount of cash kept on hand for making miscellaneous payments.
FIN-03-05	Reconciliations	Records related to the process of comparing the cash balance, as reported by the bank, with the cash balance on the company's books, and explaining any differences.
FIN-04	BUDGETS	Records related to the preparation and approval of budgets and all budget supporting material.
FIN-05	BUSINESS/FINANCAL PLANS	Records regarding a business or financial plan. A plan includes projections of fixed and variable expenses and analyses of the company's break-even point, competition, and projected sales.

Code	Name	Description
FIN-06	CONTRIBUTIONS	Records pertaining to financial contributions to charitable or not-for-profit organizations such as civic, social, or political groups. Includes United Way, Junior Achievement, sporting events, etc.
FIN-07	FINANCIAL SERVICES	Records concerning outside financial service companies such as banks, bookkeepers, CPAs, tax preparers, financial planners, insurance agents, investment advisors, and other financial consultants or contractors.
FIN-08	FINANCIAL STATEMENTS	Reports, such as the balance sheet, income statement, and statement of cash flows, that summarize the financial status and results of operations of a business.
FIN-09	INSURANCE POLICIES	Records pertaining to insurance coverage affecting company liability such as general liability, environmental liability, and property insurance. Includes policies, amendments, riders, and proofs of payment.
FIN-10	INVESTMENTS	Records pertaining to transactions and events that involve the purchase and sale of securities, property, plant, equipment, and other assets acquired for future income.
FIN-11	LOANS/CREDIT	Records pertaining to the management of loans or lines of credit obtained by the business. Includes applications and payment schedules.
FIN-12	PURCHASING	Records pertaining to the regular review of the quality of products purchased, timely delivery, and the quality of other services provided by suppliers; solicitation of bids on purchases. Includes goods and services supply source lists, policies and procedures, purchase specifications, etc. General information.
FIN-12-01	Purchase Orders	Records related to an executed document authorizing a supplier to deliver materials or equipment, or to perform services, which upon acceptance constitutes a purchase contract. Includes purchase order file, bids, and quotations.
FIN-12-02	Vendor Information	Records pertaining to product specifications, vendor and supplier files, price lists, supply sources, etc.
HR	HUMAN RESOURCES	Records regarding personnel and employment management, employee safety, and compensation and benefit issues.
HR-01	BENEFIT/PENSION PLANS	Records pertaining to business-sponsored medical and life insurance plans; pension and savings plans; ESOP plans; retirement plans. General information.
HR-01-01	Medical Plans	Records pertaining to health/medical, dental, and accident insurance plans. Includes policies, contracts, plans, and correspondence.
HR-01-02	Pension Plans	Records pertaining to pension and savings plans. Includes policies, contracts, plans, and correspondence.
HR-01-03	Workers' Compensation	Records pertaining to workers' compensation insurance. Includes policies, contracts, plans, and correspondence.
HR-02	COMPENSATION	Records pertaining to administration, determination, and monitoring of salaries and bonuses. General information.
HR-02-01	Compensation Plans	Records pertaining to salary and wage research, surveys, polices, compensation plans, and incentive plans
HR-02-02	Job Descriptions	Records pertaining to formal descriptions of the duties and responsibilities for each position in the business.
HR-03	HANDBOOK/MANUALS	Records related to communication of benefits, policies, methods, or processes to employees to ensure uniformity and compliance with company requirements. Includes employee handbooks and/or manuals.
HR-04	RECRUITMENT/STAFFING	Records related to recruitment and staffing selection. General information.
HR-04-01	Applications/Resumes	Records pertaining to hiring for an open position. Includes job description; copy of newspaper ad or job posting; list of all applicants; resumes and applications; evaluation notes; and investigation information.
HR-04-02	Temporary/Seasonal	Records pertaining to outside temporary or seasonal staffing from employment agencies or temporary employee agencies.

Code	Name	Description
HR-05	INS I-9 FORMS	Records created to comply with the INS Immigration Reform and Control Act (IRCA) of 1990. Includes I-9 forms and supporting documents.
HR-06	ORGANIZATION CHARTS	Organizational charts and supporting documentation.
HR-07	PERSONNEL	Records regarding personnel files on individual employees. General information.
HR-07-01	Employee Files	Individual employee records pertaining to personal information; salary and wage information; work history; attendance; company policy acknowledgements; performance reviews; resumes and applications; training; and termination.
HR-07-02	Employee Confidential Files	Individual employee confidential records pertaining to pre-employment references and investigations; EEO/affirmative action issues; grievances and investigations; and legal actions.
HR-07-03	Reports	Periodic or special reports pertaining to labor, personnel, and/or staffing.
HR-08	EMPLOYEE DEVELOPMENT	Records pertaining to job-related training, professional development, and continuing education programs.
HR-09	SAFETY/HEALTH	Records pertaining to training, monitoring, inspection, testing of equipment, work-safety conditions, and industrial hygiene. General information.
HR-09-01	Compliance	Records pertaining to compliance with state and federal OSHA/safety agency regulations.
HR-09-02	Inspections	Records pertaining to safety inspections of facilities and/or equipment.
HR-09-03	Employee Confidential Medical Files	Individual employee confidential records pertaining to general medical information. Includes injury records, compensation records, fitness for duty, positive drug results, medical claims forms, and doctors' reports.
HR-09-04	Employee Confidential Medical Files/Exposure	Individual employee confidential records pertaining to exposure information. Includes exposure records and doctors' reports.
HR-09-05	Training	Records pertaining to safety and health training.
HR-10	LABOR RELATIONS	Records related to relations with labor unions, including special benefits and vacations, grievances, and strike policies and procedures.
IT	INFORMATION TECHNOLOGY	Records pertaining to information technology (IT) and systems.
IT-01	SYSTEMS/DOCUMENTATION	Records pertaining to IT documentation and systems, including planning, user manuals, operating manuals, licenses, and proofs of purchase. General information.
IT-01-01	Hardware	Records pertaining to hardware documentation, including user manuals, operating manuals, licenses, proofs of purchase. Includes computers, drivers, printers, input devices, recording devices, readers, scanners, off-line or near-line storage devices.
IT-01-02	ISP	Records pertaining to Internet service providers (ISP) documentation. Includes user manuals, operating manuals, licenses, and passwords.
IT-01-03	Network	Records pertaining to network design and installation. Includes manuals, specifications, documentation, system design, layout, etc.
IT-01-04	Software	Records pertaining to application and operating software, including user manuals, operating manuals, licenses, and proofs of purchase.
IT-01-05	Telecommunications	Records pertaining to telephony systems, including user manuals, operating manuals, licenses. Includes telephones and voice-mail systems.
IT-02	WEB DEVELOPMENT/ E-COMMERCE	Records pertaining to Web development and Web services. Includes account administration, site administration, commerce tools, site statistics, etc.
IT-03	TRAINING	Records pertaining to IT training, including information on training classes and training materials.
LEG	LEGAL	Records pertaining to legal compliance and obligations of the business or corporation.
LEG-01	CONTRACTS/AGREEMENTS	Records pertaining to legal contracts and agreements. General information.

Code	Name	Description
LEG-01-01	General	Records pertaining to general contracts and agreements. Includes purchase or sale of goods or products (per the Uniform Commercial Code (UCC)); customer/client agreements; employee agreements; services/consultant/contractor agreements; distributor contracts; confidentiality agreements; equipment lease agreements; parts/components agreements; supply agreements. Includes correspondence, drafts, amendments, and payment obligations.
LEG-01-02	Warranty	Records pertaining to product and service warranties and guarantees such as service contracts and agreements provided by the business.
LEG-02	CORRESPONDENCE - LEGAL	Correspondence, memos, notes, announcements.
LEG-03	INTELLECTUAL PROPERTY	Records pertaining to the preparation, filing, and maintenance of patents, trademarks, trade names, and copyrights.
LEG-04	LITIGATION/CLAIMS	Records pertaining to allegations, claims, lawsuits, litigation, judgments, and other activities for or against the business. Records include labor grievances, insurance claims, court orders, and documents produced in the course of litigation.
LEG-05	OUTSIDE COUNSEL	Records pertaining to outside counsel for support on business law, corporate law, litigation, labor law, etc. Includes correspondence, research, legal advice, and legal opinions by outside counsel.
LEG-06	PERMITS/LICENSES	Records pertaining to the permits and licenses required for the business such as business licenses, use permits, environmental permits, etc. Includes applications, renewals, correspondence, notices, reports, etc.
LEG-07	REAL PROPERTY	Records pertaining to buying and selling of real property. General information.
LEG-07-01	Deeds/Titles	Records pertaining to business property deeds and titles. Includes property information, sale information, and background information.
LEG-07-02	Easements/Right of Ways	Records pertaining to easements, permits, and right-of-ways for real property.
LEG-07-03	Leases	Records pertaining to business property leases. Includes property information, lease information, and background information.
MS	MARKETING & SALES	Records pertaining to advertising, promotion, marketing, public relations, publicity, and sales of a product or service.
MS-01	CONTACT MANAGEMENT	Records pertaining to managing business contacts and relationships. Includes contact phone book, client database, appointment scheduling, calendar, mailing lists, and customer relationship management (CRM).
MS-02	DISTRIBUTORS	Records pertaining to outside sources for material distribution. Includes correspondence, promotions, announcements, etc.
MS-03	EVENTS	Records pertaining to events used to promote the business such as booth displays, tradeshow exhibits, workshops, and lectures. Includes event descriptions, event contacts, correspondence, announcements, ticket distribution, etc.
MS-04	MARKET RESEARCH	Records pertaining to the process of collecting and analyzing information about the potential market for the distribution and/or support of products and/or services.
MS-05	MARKET PLAN	Records pertaining to the planning and forecasting of products or services. Includes revenue forecasts, market analysis, pricing strategy, product analysis, cost studies, surveys, and product or service studies.
MS-06	INDUSTRY COMPETITION	Records pertaining to monitoring industry progress and competitor developments.
MS-06-01	Press Clippings/Trade Articles	Records pertaining to public information from newspapers, press releases, journals, magazines, etc., collected on industry and/or competitor-related information.
MS-07	PROMOTIONS	Records pertaining to a sales or advertising campaign, designed to increase visibility or sales of a product or service.
MS-07-01	Advertising	Records pertaining to advertising campaigns of company products or services.
MS-07-02	Promotional Materials	Sales promotion materials consisting of brochures, pamphlets, manuals, product models, and displays, Web site promotions, etc., for the primary purpose of promoting a company's products and/or services to customers or prospective customers.

Code	Name	Description
MS-08	PUBLIC RELATIONS/PUBLICITY	Records pertaining to efforts to publicize or promote the status of the business to the public. Includes publicity plans, press releases, announcements, newsletters, etc. (For specific product or services promotions, see Sales.) General information.
MS-08-01	Newsletters	Records pertaining to newsletters on business-related information, produced for distribution to customers, prospective customers, interested parties, etc.
MS-08-02	Press Releases	Records pertaining to press releases written for distribution to various types of public and professional media.
MS-09	SALES	Records pertaining to sale and promotion of company products or services. Records include sales reports, customer proposals or bids, promotional materials, Web site commerce, etc.
MS-09-01	Bids/Proposals	Records pertaining to bids, proposals, and quotes in response to informal requests and to formal requests such as request for proposals (RFP). General information.
MS-09-02	Orders	Records pertaining to customer orders, order acknowledgements.
MS-09-03	Price Lists	Records pertaining to pricing, price lists.
MS-09-04	Reports	Periodic or special sales and/or sales statistics reports.
OP	OPERATIONS	Records pertaining to engineering and planning; manufacturing, production and/or installation; quality-control product safety and warranties; and distribution.
OP-01	ENVIRONMENTAL HEALTH	Records pertaining to environmental and/or consumer health issues such as consumer safety, hazardous materials, emissions, noise pollution. Includes reports, responses, analyses, etc. [See HR-09 for employee health issues.]
OP-01-01	Reports/Allegations	Records pertaining to reports or allegations of environmental and/or consumer health and safety issues.
OP-02	PRODUCTS	Production records, including technical plans/documents; materials management, production control, etc.
OP-02-01	Reports/Status	Periodic or special reports on production activity and status.
OP-02-02	Work Orders	Records relating to product or production work orders.
OP-03	SERVICE/WARRANTY	Records pertaining to service or warranty maintenance on products or services, including claims, correspondence, follow-ups, resolutions, etc. (See also LEG-01-02 for warranty contracts.)
OP-03-01	Claims/Requests	Records pertaining to service or warranty claims, work orders, requests, etc. Includes follow-ups and resolutions.
OP-03-02	Reports	Periodic or special reports on service and/or warranty activity.
OP-04	INSTALLATION/ TRANSPORTATION/SHIPPING	Records pertaining to product installation, transportation, or shipping. General information.
OP-04-01	Bills of lading	Shipping bills of lading and related documents.
OP-04-02	Exports	Records pertaining to products sent to foreign countries, including orders, packing lists, correspondence, as well as any other relevant documents.
OP-04-03	Packing Lists	Shipping packing lists and related documents.
OP-04-04	Shipping	Records pertaining to shipping. Includes permits, tracking forms, reports, logs, etc.
OP-05	QUALITY	Records pertaining to product and production quality.
OP-05-01	Quality Control	Records pertaining to total quality control (TQC) program management, including monitoring, testing, inspecting, measuring, calibrating, etc.
RR	REFERENCE/RESEARCH	Data and information gathered for research and reference, including standards and studies.
RR-01	REFERENCE	Data and information gathered for research and reference. General information.
RR-01-01	Industry	Data and information pertaining to general industry practices gathered for research and reference.

Code	Name	Description
RR-01-02	Management	Data and information pertaining to general business practices gathered for research and reference.
RR-01-03	IT	Data and information pertaining to information technology (IT) gathered for research and reference.
RR-02	RESEARCH & DEVELOPMENT	Records pertaining to tasks related to the application of scientific or technical knowledge in the forecasting, planning, and developing of new products, product components, processes, or improvements. General information.
RR-02-01	Product Development	Records pertaining to research and development of new products.
RR-02-02	Technical Papers/References	Research and development papers created or collected that pertain to products. Includes white papers, technical reports, engineering reports, or notebooks.
RR-03	STANDARDS	Standards for industry type.

Sample Inventory Worksheets

A portion of a completed inventory worksheet is shown in Figure 3.3, on page 13.

ACCOUNTING Records pertaining to fiscal recordkeeping practices, records of transactions used as the basis for recording accounting entries. Includes invoices, check stubs, receipts, and similar business papers.

✔	Category	Container	Media	File Arrangement	Dates	Access
	Accounts Payable					
	Invoices					
	Expense Accounts					
	Reports					
	Ledger/Register					
	Accounts Receivable					
	Billing					
	Reports					
	Collections					
	Cash Management					
	Journal					
	Cost Accounting					
	General Ledger					

ACCOUNTING Records pertaining to fiscal recordkeeping practices, records of transactions used as the basis for recording accounting entries. Includes invoices, check stubs, receipts, and similar business papers.

✔	Category	Container	Media	File Arrangement	Dates	Access
	Journals					
	Subledgers					
	Supporting Documents					
	Payroll					
	Payroll/Registers					
	Time Sheets					
	Reports					
	Taxes					
	Income					
	Payroll					
	Property					
	Sales					
	Self-Employment					

ADMINISTRATION Records pertaining to the planning, supervising, and managing of the daily activities of the business.

✔	Category	Container	Media	File Arrangement	Dates	Access
	Correspondence/ General					
	Calendars/Schedules					
	Meetings/Reports					
	Memberships					
	Equipment/Furniture					
	Inventory Lists					
	Maintenance					
	Manuals					
	Warranties					
	Facilities					
	Building Maintenance					
	Security					
	Space Planning					

ADMINISTRATION Records pertaining to the planning, supervising, and managing of the daily activities of the business.

✔	Category	Container	Media	File Arrangement	Dates	Access
	Forms/Supplies					
	Policy and Procedures					
	Records Management					
	Manuals					
	Retention Schedule					
	Vendors					
	Consultants					
	Contractors/Subcontractors					
	Office Functions					
	Presentation Materials					
	Reference					

CLIENT RELATIONS Records pertaining to management of clients or customers regarding the sale of products and/or services.

✔	Category	Container	Media	File Arrangement	Dates	Access
	Clients/Accounts					
	Projects/Special Projects					
	Complaints					

CORPORATE Records pertaining to corporation organization and governance.

✔	Category	Container	Media	File Arrangement	Dates	Access
	Articles of Incorporation/ Bylaws					
	Board of Directors					
	Minutes/Meetings					
	Committees/Meetings					
	Shareholders					
	Annual Reports					
	SEC Reports					
	Stocks					
	Dividend Records					

FINANCE Records pertaining to fiscal management of assets, liabilities, funds, and investments.

✔	Category	Container	Media	File Arrangement	Dates	Access
	Assets					
	Fixed Assets					
	Depreciation					
	Inventory					
	Audits					
	Internal					
	External					
	Banking					
	Statements					
	Canceled Checks					
	Foreign Accounts					
	Petty Cash Fund					
	Reconciliations					

FINANCE Records pertaining to fiscal management of assets, liabilities, funds, and investments.

✔	Category	Container	Media	File Arrangement	Dates	Access
	Budgets					
	Business/Financial Plans					
	Contributions					
	Financial Services					
	Financial Statements					
	Insurance Policies					
	Investments					
	Loans/Credit					
	Purchasing					
	Purchase Orders					
	Vendor Information					

HUMAN RESOURCES Records regarding personnel and employment management, employee safety, and compensation and benefit issues.

✔	Category	Container	Media	File Arrangement	Dates	Access
	Benefit/Pension Plans					
	Medical Plans					
	Pension Plans					
	Workers' Compensation					
	Compensation					
	Plans					
	Job Descriptions					
	Handbook/Manuals					
	Recruitment/Staffing					
	Applications/Resumes					
	Temporary/Seasonal					
	INS I-9 Forms					
	Organization Charts					

HUMAN RESOURCES Records regarding personnel and employment management, employee safety, and compensation and benefit issues.

✔	Category	Container	Media	File Arrangement	Dates	Access
	Personnel					
	Employee Files					
	Employee Confidential Files					
	Reports					
	Employee Development					
	Safety/Health					
	Compliance					
	Inspections					
	Employee Confidential Medical Files					
	Training					
	Labor Relations					

INFORMATION TECHNOLOGY Records pertaining to information technology (IT) and systems.

✔	Category	Container	Media	File Arrangement	Dates	Access
	Systems/Documentation					
	Hardware					
	ISP					
	Network					
	Software					
	Telecommunications					
	Web Development/ E-Commerce					
	Training					

LEGAL Records pertaining to legal compliance and obligations of the business or corporation.

✔	Category	Container	Media	File Arrangement	Dates	Access
	Contracts/Agreements					
	General					
	Warranty					
	Correspondence – Legal					
	Intellectual Property					
	Litigation/Claims					
	Outside Counsel					
	Permits/Licenses					
	Real Property					
	Deeds/Titles					
	Easements/Right of Ways					
	Leases					

MARKETING AND SALES Records pertaining to advertising, promotion, marketing, public relations, publicity, and sales of a product or service.

✔	Category	Container	Media	File Arrangement	Dates	Access
	Contact Management					
	Distributors					
	Events					
	Market Research					
	Market Plan					
	Industry Competition					
	Press Clippings/ Trade Articles					
	Promotions					
	Advertising					
	Promotional Materials					
	Public Relations/Publicity					
	Newsletters					
	Press Releases					

MARKETING AND SALES Records pertaining to advertising, promotion, marketing, public relations, publicity, and sales of a product or service.

✔	Category	Container	Media	File Arrangement	Dates	Access
	Sales					
	Bids/Proposals					
	Orders					
	Price Lists					
	Reports					

OPERATIONS Records pertaining to engineering and planning; manufacturing, production and/or installation; quality-control product safety and warranties; and distribution.

✔	Category	Container	Media	File Arrangement	Dates	Access
	Environmental Health					
	Reports/Allegations					
	Products					
	Reports/Status					
	Work Orders					
	Service/Warranty					
	Claims/Requests					
	Reports					
	Installation/ Transportation/Shipping					
	Bills of lading					
	Exports					
	Packing Lists					
	Shipping					

OPERATIONS Records pertaining to engineering and planning; manufacturing, production and/or installation; quality-control product safety and warranties; and distribution.

✔	Category	Container	Media	File Arrangement	Dates	Access
	Quality					
	Quality Control					

REFERENCE/RESEARCH Data and information gathered for research and reference, including standards and studies.

✔	Category	Container	Media	File Arrangement	Dates	Access
	Reference					
	Industry					
	Management					
	IT					
	Research & Development					
	Product Development					
	Technical Papers/ References					
	Standards					

Model Regulatory Research Report

The following federal citations are made available as a convenience. Reliance on any such information is at the user's own risk. The accuracy, reliability, completeness, or timeliness of any information is not warranted. This report is not intended to represent legal or other professional advice. If you have specific issues regarding these citations, you are advised to discuss them with your attorney or your accountant. The information presented within this text is subject to change without notice.

Code	Citation	Agency	Records Summary	Retention Period
	Accounting, Finance, and Tax			
AFT-01	26 CFR 1.57-5(a)	Internal Revenue Service, Department of the Treasury	Records of amounts expended and adjustments made to property acquired and held for investment or to verify excessive use of qualified stock option plan.	Indefinite
AFT-02	26 CFR 1.57-5(b)	Internal Revenue Service, Department of the Treasury	Net operating losses.	Indefinite
AFT-03	26CFR1.162-17	Internal Revenue Service, Department of the Treasury	Records to substantiate ordinary and necessary business expenses of travel, transportation, and entertainment concerning the performance of services as an employee.	Not specified
AFT-04	26 CFR 1.170A-13	Internal Revenue Service, Department of the Treasury	Deductions for charitable contributions.	Not specified
AFT-05	26 CFR 1.274-5	Internal Revenue Service, Department of the Treasury	Records to substantiate ordinary and necessary business expenses of travel, entertainment, and gifts.	Not specified
AFT-06	26 CFR 1.312-15	Internal Revenue Service, Department of the Treasury	Corporations using different methods of depreciation for taxable income and escrow and payments to compute adjusted basis of property in each account.	Not specified
AFT-07	26 CFR 1.561-2	Internal Revenue Service, Department of the Treasury	Canceled dividend checks and receipts.	Indefinite
AFT-08	26 CFR 1.6001-1	Internal Revenue Service, Department of the Treasury	Books of account or records of all taxpayers, except farmers and wage earners, including inventories, as are sufficient to establish the amount of gross income, deductions, credits, or other matters.	Not specified
AFT-09	26 CFR 1.6107-1	Internal Revenue Service, Department of the Treasury	Income tax return preparers - returns.	3 years
AFT-10	26 CFR 31.3401(a)-1	Internal Revenue Service, Department of the Treasury	Employment taxes, withholding and deduction records, with respect to sick pay made directly to employees under wage continuation plan.	4 years
AFT-11	26 CFR 31.6001-1	Internal Revenue Service, Department of the Treasury	Employment tax documents, including returns, schedules, statements, and reports.	4 years
AFT-12	26 USC § 6501	Internal Revenue Service, Department of the Treasury	Limitations on assessment and collection. Receipts, canceled checks or other proof of payment and other records to support deductions or credits claimed on the return.	3 years from date the return was filed (unless fraud or substantial underreporting of income is involved).
AFT-13	26 CFR 301.6501(a)-1(a)	Internal Revenue Service, Department of the Treasury	Period of limitations upon assessment and collection.	3 years
AFT-14	26 CFR 301.6501(c)-1(a)	Internal Revenue Service, Department of the Treasury	Exceptions to general period of limitations on assessment and collection on false or fraudulent returns.	Indefinite
AFT-15	26 CFR 301.6501(e)-1(a)	Internal Revenue Service, Department of the Treasury	Limitations on assessment and collection, omissions from the gross income.	6 years

Code	Citation	Agency	Records Summary	Retention Period
AFT-16	29 CFR 516(5)	Employment Standards Administration, Department of Labor, Wage and Hour Division Fair Labor Standards Act	Employers: payroll records; certificates, agreements, plans, notices, etc.; and sales and purchase records. *Applies to all employers.*	3 years
AFT-17	29 CFR 516(6)	Employment Standards Administration, Department of Labor, Wage and Hour Division Fair Labor Standards Act	Wage rate tables; order, shipping, and billing records; records of additions to or deductions from wages paid. *Applies to all employers.*	2 years
AFT-18	29 USC § 211	Wage and Hour Division, Department of Labor Fair Labor Standards Act of 1938	Wages, hours, and other conditions and practices of employment.	Not specified
AFT-19	29 CFR 825.500	Employment Standards Administration, Department of Labor Family Medical Leave Act (FMLA)	Basic payroll data; daily or weekly hours worked per pay period; additions to or deductions from wages; and total compensation paid. *Applies to employers with 50 or more employees.*	3 years
AFT-20	29 CFR 1620.32	Equal Employment Opportunity Commission, Department of Labor Equal Pay Act of 1963	All records as in 29 CFR 516, and other matters which describe or explain the basis for payment of any wage differential to employees of the opposite sex in the same establishment, and which may be pertinent to a determination whether such differential is based on a factor other than sex. *Applies to all employers.*	2 years
AFT-21	29 CFR 1627.3(a)	Equal Employment Opportunity Commission, Department of Labor Age Discrimination in Employment Act (ADEA) of 1967	Payroll records for each employee. *Applies to employers with 20 or more employees.*	3 years
AFT-22	31 CFR 103.32	Department of the Treasury	Foreign financial accounts.	5 years
AFT-23	31 CFR 501.601	Office of Foreign Assets Control, Department of the Treasury	Foreign assets – record of each such transaction.	5 years
Consumer Safety				
CS-01	15 USC § 2607	Commerce and Trade	Control of Toxic Substances Records of significant adverse reactions to health or the environment.	30 years from the date such reactions were first known
CS-02	15 USC § 2607	Commerce and Trade	Control of Toxic Substances Records of consumer allegations of personal injury or harm to health, reports of occupational disease or injury, and reports or complaints of injury to the environment submitted to the manufacturer, processor, or distributor in commerce from any source.	5 years from the date first known

Employment, Personnel, and Benefit Records

Code	Citation	Agency	Records Summary	Retention Period
EPB-01	8 CFR 274a	Immigration and Naturalization Service, Department of Justice	I-9 Forms. *Applies to employers of 1 or more employees.*	Hire plus 3 years or Termination plus one, whichever is later
EPB-02	8 USC 1324a	Immigration and Naturalization Service, U.S. Justice Department. Immigration Reform and Control Act (IRCA) of 1990	I-9 Forms. *Applies to employers of 1 or more employees.*	Hire plus 3 years or Termination plus one, whichever is later
EPB-03	29 CFR 405.9	Office of Labor-Management Standards, Department of Labor. Labor-Management Reporting and Disclosure Act of 1959	Labor-Management Reporting. Employer records.	5 years
EPB-04	29 CFR 516(5)	Employment Standards Administration, Department of Labor, Wage and Hour Division. Fair Labor Standards Act	Employers: payroll records and certificates, agreements, plans, notices, etc. *Applies to all employers.*	3 years
EPB-05	29 CFR 516(6)	Employment Standards Administration, Department of Labor, Wage and Hour Division. Fair Labor Standards Act	Basic employment and earnings records; wage rate tables; order, shipping, and billing records; records of additions to or deductions from wages paid. *Applies to all employers.*	2 years
EPB-06	29 CFR 1602.14	Equal Employment Opportunity Commission, Department of Labor. Title VII of the Civil Rights Act of 1991	Personnel or employment records and involuntary termination records. *Applies to employers with 15 or more employees.*	1 year
EPB-07	29 CFR 1602.14	Equal Employment Opportunity Commission, Department of Labor	Records pertaining to a discrimination charge or action against an employer under Title VII or the ADA. *Applies to employers with 15 or more employees.*	Until final disposition of the charge or the action
EPB-08	29 CFR 1602.21	Equal Employment Opportunity Commission, Department of Labor. Title VII of the Civil Rights Act of 1991	Apprenticeship application records. *Applies to employers with 15 or more employees.*	2 years
EPB-09	29 CFR 1602.21(b)	Equal Employment Opportunity Commission, Department of Labor. Title VII of the Civil Rights Act of 1991	Records pertaining to a discrimination charge or action against an employer under Apprenticeship applications. *Applies to employers with 15 or more employees.*	Until final disposition of the charge or the action
EPB-10	29 CFR 1620.32	Equal Employment Opportunity Commission, Department of Labor. Equal Pay Act of 1963	All records as in 29 CFR 516, and other matters that describe or explain the basis for payment of any wage differential to employees of the opposite sex in the same establishment and that may be pertinent to a determination whether such differential is based on a factor other than sex. *Applies to all employers.*	2 years
EPB-11	29 CFR 1627.3(b)	Equal Employment Opportunity Commission, Department of Labor. Age Discrimination in Employment Act (ADEA) of 1967	Employment records. *Applies to employers with 20 or more employees.*	1 year

Code	Citation	Agency	Records Summary	Retention Period
EPB-12	29 CFR 1627.3(b)(2)	Equal Employment Opportunity Commission, Department of Labor; Age Discrimination in Employment Act (ADEA) of 1967	Employee benefit plans and any seniority systems and merit systems. *Applies to employers with 20 or more employees.*	Full period the plan or system is in effect, and at least 1 year after termination
EPB-13	29 USC § 211	Department of Labor, Wage and Hour Division	Data regarding the wages, hours, and other conditions and practices of employment.	Not specified
EPB-14	29 USC § 623	Equal Employment Opportunity Commission, Department of Labor	Age Discrimination In Employment	Not specified
EPB-15	29 USC § 1027	Employment Standards Administration, Department of Labor; Employee Retirement Income Security Act (ERISA) of 1974	Employee benefit plan. Plan documents, including vouchers, worksheets, receipts, and applicable resolutions.	6 years after filing
Export Records				
EX-01	15 CFR 30.11	Bureau of the Census, Department of Commerce and Foreign Trade; Customs Service	Export documents, orders, packing lists, correspondence, as well as any other relevant documents.	3 years
EX-02	19 CFR 10.308	United States Customs Service, Department of the Treasury	Importer: certifications of origin. Exporter: (to Canada) certifications of origin.	5 years
Legal				
LG-01	17 USC § 507	Copyright Infringement and Remedies	Limitations on actions.	Criminal Proceedings - 5 years; Civil Actions - 3 years
LG-02	35 USC § 286	Patent and Trademark Office	Filing of the complaint or counterclaim for patent infringement - time limitation.	6 years
Occupational Safety and Health				
OSH-01	29 CFR 1904.2 1904.4 1904.5 1904.6	Occupational Safety and Health Administration, Department of Labor; Occupational Safety and Health Act (OSHA) of 1970	Occupational injuries and illnesses logs and summaries; supplemental records; and posted annual summaries.	5 years
OSH-02	29 CFR 1910.940	Occupational Safety and Health Administration, Department of Labor (effective 01/01/02)	Occupational injuries - ergonomics - employee reports and responses, job hazard analyses and controls, records of quick-fix controls. *Applies to employers with 10 or more employees.*	5 years
OSH-03	29 CFR 1910.940	Occupational Safety and Health Administration, Department of Labor (effective 01/01/02)	Occupational injuries - ergonomics - material safety data (MSD) management records. *Applies to employers with 10 or more employees.*	Duration of injured employee's employment plus 5 years
OSH-04	29 CFR 1910.1020(d)(1)(i)	Occupational Safety and Health Administration, Department of Labor; Occupational Safety and Health Standards	Toxic and Hazardous Substances. Medical records for each employee. (Medical records of employees who have worked for less than (1) year for the employer need not be retained beyond the term of employment if they are provided to the employee upon the termination of employment.)	Duration of injured employee's employment plus 30 years

Code	Citation	Agency	Records Summary	Retention Period
OSH-05	29 CFR 1910.1020(d)(1)(ii) 29 CFR 1910.1020(d)(1)(iii)	Occupational Safety and Health Administration, Department of Labor Occupational Safety and Health Standards	Toxic and Hazardous Substances. Employee exposure records. Analyses using exposure or medical records.	30 years
OSH-06	29 USC § 657	Occupational Safety and Health, Department of Labor	Occupational Safety and Health Standards.	Not specified

Web Sites for Further Research:

Code of Federal Regulations – www.access.gpo.gov/nara/cfr/

United States Code – www4.law.cornell.edu/uscode/

U.S. Government Portal – www.firstgov.gov/

Nolo Press – www.nolo.com/

Statutes of Limitations – State Summaries

The following citations are made available as a convenience. Reliance on any such information is at the user's own risk. The accuracy, reliability, completeness, or timeliness of this information is not warranted. This information is not intended to represent legal or other professional advice. If you have specific issues regarding these citations, you are advised to discuss them with your attorney. Information presented within this text is subject to change without notice.

State	Citations	Written Contracts*	Property Damage*	Personal Injury*
Alabama	Code of Ala. § 6-2-34 § 6-2-38	6 years	6 years	2 years
Alaska	AS §09.10.070 §09.10.053	3 years	6 years	2 years
Arizona	ARS §12-542 §12-548	6 years	2 years	2 years
Arkansas	Ark. Code Ann. §16-56-105 §16-56-111	5 years	3 years	3 years
California	Cal. Civ. Proc. Code §340 §337 §338	4 years	3 years	1 years
Colorado	CRS §13-80-102 §13-80-101	3 years	2 years	2 years
Connecticut	Conn. Gen. Stat. Ann. §52-576 §52-584	6 years	2 years	2 years
Delaware	Del. Code Ann. Title 10, §8107 Title 10, §8119 Title 10, §8106	3 years	2 years	2 years

* Review statutes for more detail.

State	Citations	Written Contracts*	Property Damage*	Personal Injury*
District of Columbia	D.C. Code §12-301	3 years	3 years	3 years
Florida	Fla. Stat. Ann. §95.11(2) §95.11(3)	5	4	4
Georgia	Ga. Code Ann. §9-3-24 §9-3-30 §9-3-33	6	4	2
Hawaii	HRS §657-1 §657-7	6	2	2
Idaho	Id. Code §5-216 §5-218 §5-219	5	3	2
Illinois	Ill. Comp. Stat. 735 ILCS 5/13-206 735 ILCS 5/13-202	10	5	2
Indiana	Ind. Code Ann. §34-11-2-4 §34-11-2-7 §34-11-2-9	10	2 or 6 years*	2
Iowa	Iowa Code Ann. §614.1(2) §614.1(5) §614.1(6)	10	5	2
Kansas	KSA §60-511(1) §60-513 §60-513(a)(2)	5	2	2
Kentucky	KRS §413.090(2) §413.120 §413.125 §413.140(1)	15	2 or 5 years*	1
Louisiana	La. Civil Code §3492 §3499	10	1	1
Maine	Me. Rev. Stat. Ann. tit. 14§752	6	6	6
Maryland	Md. Courts & Jud. Proc. Code Ann. §5-101	3	3	3
Massachusetts	MGL c.260, §2 c.260, §2A c.260, §4	6	3	3
Michigan	MCL §600.5805(8) §600.5807(8)	6	3	3

* Review statutes for more detail.

State	Citations	Written Contracts*	Property Damage*	Personal Injury*
Minnesota	Minn. Stat. Ann. §541.05(1) §541.05(4) §541.05(5)	6	6	6
Mississippi	Miss. Code. Ann. §15-1-49	3	3	3
Missouri	MRS §516.110 §516.120	5 or 10*	5	5
Montana	MCA §27-2-202 §27-2-204 §27-2-207	8	2	3
Nebraska	Neb. Rev. Stat. §25-205 §25-207	5	4	4
Nevada	NRS §11.190(1)(b) §11.190(3)(c) §11.190(4)(e)	6	3	2
New Hampshire	N.H. RSA §508:4	3	3	3
New Jersey	N.J. Stat. Ann. §2A:14-1 §2A:14-2	6	6	2
New Mexico	N.M. Stat. Ann. §37-1-3 §37-1-4 §37-1-8	6	4	3
New York	N.Y. Civ. Prac. Laws & Rules §213 §214	6	3	3
North Carolina	N.C. Gen. Stat. §1-52(1) §1-52(16)	3	3	3
North Dakota	N.D. Cent. Code §28-01-16(1) §28-01-16(4) §28-01-16(5)	6	6	6
Ohio	ORC §2305.06 §2305.10	15	2	2
Oklahoma	Okla. Stat. Ann. t.12, §95(1) t.12, §95(3)	5	2	2
Oregon	ORS §12.080 §12.110	6	6	2

* Review statutes for more detail.

State	Citations	Written Contracts*	Property Damage*	Personal Injury*
Pennsylvania	42 Pa. Cons. Stat. Ann. §5524(2) §5524(3) §5525(3),(8)	4	2	2
Rhode Island	R.I. Gen. Laws §9-1-13(a) §9-1-14(b)	10	10	3
South Carolina	S.C. Code Ann. §15-3-530(1) §15-3-530(2), (3) §15-3-530(5)	3	3	3
South Dakota	S.D. Codified Laws Ann. §15-2-13(1) §15-2-13(4) §15-2-14(3)	6	6	3
Tennessee	Tenn. Code Ann. §28-3-104 §28-3-105 §28-3-109	6	3	1
Texas	Tex. Civ. Prac. & Rem. Code §16.003 §16.004	4	2	2
Utah	Utah Code Ann. §78-12-23 §78-12-25 §78-12-26	6	3	4
Vermont	Vt. Stat. Ann. t.12, §511 t.12, §512	6	3	3
Virginia	Va. Code Ann. §8.01-243 §8.01-243(2) §8.01-246(2)	5	5	2
Washington	RCW §4.16.040 §4.16.080 §4.16.080(2)	6	3	3
West Virginia	W. Va. Code §55-2-6 §55-2-12(a) §55-2-12(b)	10	2	2
Wisconsin	Wis. Stat. Ann. §893.43 §893.52 §893.54(1)	6	6	3
Wyoming	Wyo. Stat. §1-3-105(a)(i) §1-3-105(a)(iv)(b) §1-3-105(a)(iv)(c)	10	4	4

* Review statutes for more detail.

Model Retention Schedule

This Model Retention Schedule is based on common business records. The information is made available as a convenience. Reliance on any such information is at the user's own risk. The accuracy, reliability, completeness, or timeliness of any information is not warranted. This information is not intended to represent legal or other professional advice. If you have specific issues regarding the information provided, you are advised to discuss them with your attorney or your accountant. Information presented within this text is subject to change without notice.

Retention Period Abbreviations

ACT (Active): Keep while active and until matter is terminated, closed, or completed, e.g., while the contract is in effect, the insurance policy is in force, you own the property, the license is valid, etc.
AR (Annual Review): Review periodically to determine if material is still current and up-to-date.
ATA (After Tax or Audit): Keep until tax filing date or final audit completed.
C (Creation): Point of creation.
CY (Current Year): Current calendar or fiscal year.
Y (Years): Number of years.
IND (Indefinite): Keep for an open-ended time period.
SUP (Superseded): Keep until obsolete and/or replaced.
+ (Plus): Add the components, e.g., CY+4Y = Current year plus four years, C+1Y = Point of creation plus one year.
SC (State Considerations): Considerations of state statutes that may influence retention requirements.

Category		Regulatory Research		Retention Period
ACC	ACCOUNTING	Codes	Retention Period	Keep
ACC-01	ACCOUNTS PAYABLE			CY+5Y
ACC-01-01	Invoices	AFT-08 AFT-12 AFT-13	Not specified 3 Y 3 Y	CY+5Y
ACC-01-02	Expense Accounts	AFT-03 or AFT-05	Not specified	CY+5Y
ACC-01-03	Contributions	AFT-04, AFT-06 AFT-13	Not Specified 3 Y	CY+5Y
ACC-01-04	Ledger	AFT-08	Indefinite	CY+5Y
ACC-01-05	Reports			CY+5Y
ACC-02	ACCOUNTS RECEIVABLE			CY+5Y

	Category		Regulatory Research		Retention Period
ACC-02-01	Billing	AFT-16	2 Y		CY+5Y
ACC-02-02	Reports				CY+5Y
ACC-02-03	Collections	AFT-13	3 Y		CY+5Y
ACC-03	CASH MANAGEMENT				CY+5Y
ACC-03-01	Journal	AFT-08 AFT-12	Not specified 3 Y		CY+5Y
ACC-04	COST ACCOUNTING				CY+5Y
ACC-04-01	Cost Ledger	AFT-08 AFT-12	Not specified 3 Y		CY+4Y
ACC-05	GENERAL LEDGER	AFT-08	Not specified		CY+99Y
ACC-05-01	Journal	AFT-08 AFT-02	Not specified Indefinite		CY+4Y
ACC-05-02	Subledgers	AFT-08 AFT-02	Not specified Indefinite		CY+4Y
ACC-05-03	Supporting Documents	AFT-12	3 Y		CY+4Y
ACC-06	PAYROLL	AFT-16, AFT-21 AFT-20	3 Y 2 Y		CY+4Y
ACC-06-01	Payroll/Registers	AFT-16, AFT-21 AFT-20	3 Y 2 Y		CY+4Y
ACC-06-02	Reports				CY+4Y
ACC-06-03	Time Sheets	AFT-17	2 Y		CY+4Y
ACC-06-04	W-2 Forms	AFT-17			CY+4Y
ACC-06-05	W-4 Forms	AFT-17			CY+4Y
ACC-07	TAX COMPLIANCE				CY+4Y
ACC-07-01	Income Tax Returns	AFT-08, AFT-04 AFT-12, AFT-13	Not specified 3 Y		CY+5Y
ACC-07-02	Payroll/Employment Tax Returns	AFT-11	4 Y		CY+5Y
ACC-07-03	Property Tax Returns	AFT-08 AFT-12, AFT-13	Not specified 3 Y		CY+5Y
ACC-07-04	Sales Tax Returns	AFT-08	Not specified		CY+5Y
ACC-07-05	Self-Employment Tax Returns	AFT-08 AFT-12, AFT-13	Not specified 3 Y		CY+5Y
ADM	ADMINISTRATION	Codes	Legal Retention		Keep
ADM-01	CORRESPONDENCE/GENERAL				C+1Y
ADM-02	CALENDARS/SCHEDULES				C+1Y
ADM-03	MEETINGS/REPORTS				C+3Y
ADM-04	MEMBERSHIPS				ACT
ADM-05	EQUIPMENT/FURNITURE				ACT
ADM-05-01	Inventory Lists				ACT
ADM-05-02	Maintenance				ACT
ADM-05-03	Manuals				ACT
ADM-05-04	Warranties				ACT
ADM-06	FACILITIES				ACT
ADM-06-01	Building Maintenance				ACT
ADM-06-02	Security				ACT

	Category	Regulatory Research		Retention Period
ADM-06-03	Space Planning/Plans			ACT
ADM-07	FORMS/SUPPLIES			SUP
ADM-08	POLICY AND PROCEDURES			ACT+10Y
ADM-09	RECORDS MANAGEMENT			ACT
ADM-09-01	Policies/Procedures			ACT+10Y
ADM-09-02	Retention Schedule			ACT+10Y
ADM-10	VENDORS			ACT
ADM-11	CONSULTANTS			ACT
ADM-12	CONTRACTORS/SUBCONTRACTORS			ACT
ADM-13	OFFICE FUNCTIONS			C+1Y
ADM-14	PRESENTATION MATERIALS			ACT+3Y
ADM-15	REFERENCE			SUP
CR	CLIENT RELATIONS	Codes	Legal Retention	Keep
CR-01	CLIENTS/ACCOUNTS			ACT+6Y
CR-02	PROJECTS/SPECIAL PROJECTS			ACT+6Y
CR-03	COMPLAINTS			ACT+1Y
COR	CORPORATE	Codes	Legal Retention	Keep
COR-01	ARTICLES OF INCORPORATION/BYLAWS			ACT+99Y
COR-02	BOARD OF DIRECTORS			ACT+99Y
COR-02-01	Minutes/Meetings	SC		ACT+99Y
COR-02-02	Committees/Meetings	SC		ACT+99Y
COR-03	SHAREHOLDER RECORDS	SC		CY+10Y
COR-03-01	Annual Reports	SC		CY+99Y
COR-03-02	SEC Reports	SC		CY+10Y
COR-04	STOCK RECORDS	SC		CY+10Y
COR-04-01	Dividend Records	AFT-07		CY+10Y
FIN	FINANCE	Codes	Legal Retention	Keep
FIN-01	ASSETS			CY+4Y
FIN-01-01	Fixed Assets	AFT-08 AFT-12	Not specified 3Y	CY+4Y
FIN-01-02	Depreciation	AFT-06 AFT-13	Not Specified 3Y	CY+4Y
FIN-01-03	Inventory	AFT-08 AFT-13	Not specified 3Y	CY+4Y
FIN-02	AUDITS			CY+2Y
FIN-02-01	Internal			CY+2Y
FIN-02-02	External			CY+4Y
FIN-03	BANKING			CY+4Y
FIN-03-01	Statements			CY+3Y
FIN-03-02	Canceled Checks	AFT-04, AFT-06 AFT-13	Not Specified 3Y	CY+4Y
FIN-03-03	Foreign Accounts	AFT-22	5Y	CY+4Y
FIN-03-04	Petty Cash Fund	AFT-08 AFT-12	Not specified 3Y	CY+4Y

	Category		Regulatory Research	Retention Period
FIN-03-05	Reconciliations	AFT-08 AFT-12	Not specified 3Y	CY+3Y
FIN-04	BUDGETS			ACT+1Y
FIN-05	BUSINESS/FINANCIAL PLANS			SUP
FIN-06	FINANCIAL STATEMENTS	AFT-08 AFT-12	Not specified 3Y	CY+10Y
FIN-07	INSURANCE POLICIES			ACT+6Y
FIN-08	INVESTMENTS	AFT-08 AFT-12	Not specified 3Y	ACT+5Y
FIN-09	LOANS/CREDIT	AFT-08 AFT-12	Not specified 3Y	ACT+6Y
FIN-10	PURCHASING			CY+4Y
FIN-10-01	Purchase Orders			CY+4Y
FIN-10-02	Vendor Information			ACT
HR	HUMAN RESOURCES	Codes	Legal Retention	Keep
HR-01	BENEFIT/PENSION PLANS			ACT+6Y
HR-01-01	Medical Plans	EPB-12 EPB-15	In effect+1Y 6Y	ACT+6Y
HR-01-02	Pension Plans	EPB-12 EPB-15	In effect+1Y 6Y	ACT+6Y
HR-01-03	Workers' Compensation			ACT+6Y
HR-02	COMPENSATION			ACT+4Y
HR-02-01	Compensation Plans	EPB-05, EPB-10 EPB-13	2Y Not specified	ACT+4Y
HR-02-02	Job Descriptions			ACT+4Y
HR-03	HANDBOOK/MANUALS			ACT+10Y
HR-04	RECRUITMENT/STAFFING			CY+1Y
HR-04-01	Applications/Resumes	EPB-11	1Y	CY+1Y
HR-04-02	Temporary/Seasonal	EPB-11	1Y	ACT
HR-05	INS I-9 FORMS	EPB-01 EPB-02	3Y 3Y	C+3Y
HR-06	ORGANIZATION CHARTS			ACT
HR-07	PERSONNEL			CY+3Y
HR-07-01	Employee Files	EPB-07 EPB-11	1Y	ACT+3Y
HR-07-02	Employee Confidential Files	EPB-09	Until disposition of charge	ACT
HR-07-03	Reports			CY+3Y
HR-08	EMPLOYEE DEVELOPMENT			CY+3YY
HR-09	SAFETY/ENVIRONMENTAL HEALTH			CY+5Y
HR-09-01	Compliance	OSH-01, OSH-02	5Y	CY+5Y
HR-09-02	Inspections			CY+5Y
HR-09-03	Employee Confidential Medical Files	OSH-01, OSH-02	5Y	ACT+5Y
HR-09-04	Employee Confidential Medical Files/ Exposure	OSH-04	30Y	ACT+30Y
HR-09-05	Training			ACT+10Y

	Category		Regulatory Research	Retention Period
HR-10	LABOR RELATIONS	EPB-03	5Y	ACT+5Y
IT	INFORMATION TECHNOLOGY	Codes	Legal Retention	Keep
IT-01	SYSTEMS/DOCUMENTATION			ACT
IT-01-01	Hardware			ACT
IT-01-02	ISP			ACT
IT-01-03	Network			ACT
IT-01-04	Software			ACT
IT-01-05	Telecommunications			ACT
IT-02	WEB DEVELOPMENT/E-COMMERCE			ACT
IT-03	TRAINING			ACT
LEG	LEGAL	Codes	Legal Retention	Keep
LEG-01	CONTRACTS/AGREEMENTS			ACT+6Y
LEG-01-01	General	SC	ACT+6Y	ACT+6Y
LEG-01-02	Warranty	SC	ACT+6Y	ACT+6Y
LEG-02	CORRESPONDENCE - LEGAL			CY+1Y
LEG-03	INTELLECTUAL PROPERTY	LG-01	3Y	ACT+6Y
		LG-02	6Y	
LEG-04	LITIGATION/CLAIMS		3Y	ACT+3Y
LEG-05	OUTSIDE COUNSEL			ACT
LEG-06	PERMITS/LICENSES		ACT	ACT
LEG-07	REAL PROPERTY			ACT+6Y
LEG-07-01	Deeds/Titles	SC	ACT+6Y	ACT+6Y
LEG-07-02	Easements/Right of Ways	SC	ACT+6Y	ACT+6Y
LEG-07-03	Leases	SC	ACT+6Y	ACT+6Y
MS	MARKETING & SALES	Codes	Legal Retention	Keep
MS-01	CONTACT MANAGEMENT			ACT
MS-02	DISTRIBUTORS			ACT+3Y
MS-03	EVENTS			IND
MS-04	MARKET RESEARCH			ACT
MS-05	MARKET PLAN			ACT
MS-06	INDUSTRY COMPETITION			IND
MS-06-01	Press Clippings/Trade Articles			IND
MS-07	PROMOTIONS			CY+3Y
MS-07-01	Advertising			CY+3Y
MS-07-02	Promotional Materials			CY+3Y
MS-08	PUBLIC RELATIONS/PUBLICITY			IND
MS-08-01	Newsletters			IND
MS-08-02	Press Releases			IND
MS-09	SALES			CY+3Y
MS-09-01	Bids/Proposals			ACT+1
MS-09-02	Orders			CY+3
MS-09-03	Price Lists			SUP+10
MS-09-04	Reports			CY+3

Category		Regulatory Research		Retention Period
OP	OPERATIONS	Codes	Legal Retention	Keep
OP-01	ENVIRONMENTAL HEALTH			CY+5
OP-01-01	Reports/Allegations	CS-01	5Y	CY+5
OP-02	PRODUCTION			CY+3
OP-02-01	Reports/Status			CY+3
OP-02-02	Work Orders			CY+3
OP-03	SERVICE/WARRANTY			
OP-03-01	Claims/Requests			
OP-03-02	Reports			CY+3
OP-04	INSTALLATION/TRANSPORTATION/SHIPPING			CY+1
OP-04-01	Bills of Lading			CY+1
OP-04-02	Exports	EX-01	3Y	CY+5
		EX-02	5Y	
OP-04-03	Packing Lists			CY+2
OP-04-04	Shipping			CY+1
OP-05	QUALITY			IND
OP-05-01	Quality Control			IND
RR	REFERENCE/RESEARCH	Codes	Legal Retention	Keep
RR-01	REFERENCE			ACT
RR-01-01	Industry			ACT
RR-01-02	Management			ACT
RR-01-03	IT			ACT
RR-02	RESEARCH & DEVELOPMENT			IND
RR-02-01	Product Design/Development			IND
RR-02-01	Technical Papers/References			IND
RR-03	STANDARDS			SUP

Additional Resources

The following list of records and information management resources is not exhaustive. However, it is an example of the materials available to small business owners who need information about and assistance with records and information procedures.

Books

ARMA International. *Alphabetic Filing Rules.* 2d ed. Prairie Village, KS: ARMA International, 1995. (This publication is accredited as an American National Standard by the American National Standards Institute (ANSI). It is an authoritative treatment of standard rules for alphabetic filing with each rule described and illustrated in detail.)

_____ . *Developing and Operating a Records Retention Program—A Guideline.* Prairie Village, KS: ARMA International, 1986.

_____ . *Guideline for Managing E-mail.* Prairie Village, KS: ARMA International, 2000.

_____ . *Records and Information Management 2002 Buyer's Guide.* Prairie Village, KS: ARMA International, 2002.

Heldenbrand Morrissette, Nan. *Financial Institutions Records Retention Manual.* 4th ed. Financial Managers Society, 2001.

Jones, Virginia A., CRM, and Kris E. Keyes. *Emergency Management for Records and Information Programs.* Prairie Village, KS: ARMA International, 2001. (This essential guide will help you prepare for and recover from natural or human-caused disasters. Its five sections provide a step-by-step guide through the essential phases of emergency management—prevention, preparedness, response, and recovery—and include such topics as the basic concepts of emergency management and insights on selling it to top management; vital records; risk management; and disaster prevention planning, preparation of the emergency management plan, and recovery and resumption of operations. Checklists at the end of each chapter review major concepts and guide you in forming your emergency plan. Small Business Tips provide information of special importance to small organizations.)

Skupsky, Donald S. J.D., CRM, FAI. *Recordkeeping Requirements.* Denver: Information Requirements Clearinghouse, 1994.

_____ . *Records Retention Procedure.* Denver: Information Requirements Clearinghouse, 1995.

Software

Information Requirements Clearinghouse, *Retention Manager*™. Denver: Information Requirements Clearinghouse, 2000.

Zasio Enterprises, *Retention 6.0*™.

Internet

ARMA International. *Buyer's Guide* at www.arma.org. (The *Buyer's Guide* provides technology-related articles and vendor information.)

_____ . Books, guidelines, software, and other information are available on-line at www.arma.org/bookstore.

Glossary

active records. Records needed to perform current operations. Subject to frequent use and usually located near the user. Can be accessed manually or on-line via a computer system.

alphabetic filing arrangement. The arrangement, in alphabetic order, of records or entries.

alphanumeric. A classification system that uses a combination of letters and numbers, in combination with punctuation marks, to develop codes for classifying and retrieving information. A classification system that uses ASCII characters, numbers, and letters in that order.

caption. A title, heading, short explanation, or description of a document or record.

categories. Collections of related files that are used together and filed together. Also called *subject categories* or *subject headings*.

chronologic filing arrangement. The arrangement of records according to their dates.

classification folder. A heavy-duty pressboard folder with one or two inner dividers. The folder has fasteners on the front and back covers and double-faced fasteners on each divider. It provides four or six places to separate and file documents within one folder.

combination folder. A folder that has both a top tab, for drawer files, and a side tab, for open-shelf files.

commercial records center. A records center that stores the records of several organizations and provides services on a fee basis.

dictionary arrangement. A single alphabetic filing arrangement in which all types of entries (names, subjects, titles, etc.) are interfiled.

duplex-numeric. A coding system using numbers (or sometimes letters) with two or more parts separated by a dash, space, or comma.

electronic record. A record stored on electronic storage media that can be readily accessed or changed. Also known as a *machine-readable record*.

encyclopedic arrangement. An arrangement of filing in which records are filed under broad, major headings (categories) and then under the specific subheading (subcategory) to which they relate. Headings and subheadings are arranged alphabetically.

file categories. Collections of related files used together and filed together. See also *records series* and *subject headings*.

file folder label. The item on a folder tab that contains the name of the subject or number given to the file folder contents; may have other pertinent information, be color-coded to denote its place in an overall filing system, or have a bar code.

geographic filing arrangement. The arrangement of records by geographic location, usually arranged by numeric code or in alphabetic order.

hanging folder. A folder that has small hooks on each corner that allow it to be hung on or suspended from a frame. These folders are used to hold loose documents, odd-size documents, bound documents, etc.

inactive records. Records that do not have to be readily available, but which must be kept for legal, fiscal, or historical purposes. See also *active records*.

industry-specific categories. Categories of records maintained that are unique to the industry of the business. These records pertain to the operations and services conducted by the business and to the functions it performs in carrying out these operations and services.

jacket folder. A flat folder that is closed on three sides. It is used to hold odd-size documents, bound documents, loose documents, brochures, etc.

legal value. Value inherent in records that provide legal proof of business transactions. The value of records in demonstrating compliance with legal, statutory, and regulatory requirements.

nonrecords. Items that are not usually included within the scope of official records, e.g., convenience file, day file, reference materials, drafts, etc. They are documents not required to be retained and therefore do not appear on a records retention schedule.

numeric filing arrangement. An arrangement in which records are filed in numeric order. Any classification system for arranging records that is based on numbers.

official record. The record the business retains to meet the legal, fiscal, and/or operational retention requirements. Significant, vital, or important record of continuing value to be protected, managed, and retained according to established retention schedules. Often, but not necessarily an original. In law, an official record has the legally recognized and judicially enforceable quality of establishing some fact.

operational record. A record that documents those activities of an organization that are directed towards the substantive purpose for which the organization was created.

pocket folder. A partially enclosed folder with side-panel gussets for expansion. Some pocket folders have accordion-pleat gussets so that pockets can easily expand to hold numerous papers and documents. Expansions can range from 3/4 inches to as wide as 5 inches.

record. Recorded information, regardless of medium or characteristics, made or received by an organization that is evidence of its operation, and has value requiring its retention for a specific period of time.

records appraisal. The process of evaluating records based on their current operational, regulatory, legal, fiscal, and historical significance, their informational value, arrangement, and their relationship to other records.

records inventory. A detailed listing that could include the types, locations, dates, volumes, equipment, classification systems, and usage data of an organization's records.

records life cycle. The span of time of a record from its creation or receipt, through its useful life to its final disposition or retention as a historical record.

records retention schedule. A comprehensive list of records series titles, indicating for each series the length of time it is to be maintained. The schedule may include retention in active office areas, inactive storage areas, and when and if such series may be destroyed or formally transferred to another entity, such as an archives, for historical preservation.

records series. A group of related records filed/used together as a unit and evaluated as a unit for retention purposes.

records survey. A detailed review that gathers basic information about the quantity, type, function, location, and organization of records.

request for purchase (RFP). The soliciting document used in negotiated procurement to communicate requirements and to solicit proposals. A formal request to vendors for a formal response describing the proposed makeup and possible costs for a specific set of goods or services.

retention period. The time period records must be kept according to operational, legal, regulatory, and fiscal requirements.

standard categories. Categories of records that pertain to office maintenance functions such as personnel, facilities management, administrative (office) functions, and information technology.

statute of limitations. A period of time in which legal action can be taken. Federal, state, and provincial statutes of limitation should be considered when developing retention periods of records.

subject filing arrangement. An arrangement in which records are filed alphabetically in topic or subject order.

subject headings. Headings or categories under which groups of related records are filed.

substantive record. A correspondence document having long-term value. It contains business transaction information such as purchasing instructions or letters of agreement. Substantive correspondence is filed within a subject category that matches its contents. The retention period matches the subject category.

tab. A projection beyond the main body of a guide or folder upon which the caption appears. A tab is on the top or side of a folder.

transitory record. Routine correspondence, documents, or records with short-term value. The retention period is limited to the interval required for completion of the action covered by the communication.

vital records. Those records within a business essential to the continuation of the business if a disaster strikes. Such records are necessary to re-create the organization's legal and financial status and to determine the rights and obligations of employees, customers, stockholders, and citizens.

Index

About the Author

Teri J. Mark, CRM, has more than 20 years' experience in records and information management. As a consultant and small business owner, she worked with clients on the design, development, and implementation of total records management programs, including uniform filing classification systems, retention programs, vital records programs, workflow analysis, policies and procedures manuals, and electronic records systems.

Teri frequently speaks on records management topics before business and professional groups, and she has authored articles for professional journals. She has been a certified records manager (CRM) since 1985 and is a past regent of exam development for that certifying body, the Institute of Certified Records Managers (ICRM). She holds a Bachelor of Arts degree in Anthropology from the University of North Dakota.

Currently, Teri is serving as the State Records Manager for the State of Nevada in Carson City. She also helps her husband, Bill Davidson, manage the records of his small business. Any comments or questions may be sent to Teri at *tj_mark@yahoo.com*.

About ARMA International

ARMA International is the leading professional organization for persons in the expanding field of records and information management.

As of February 2003, ARMA has about 10,000 members in the United States, Canada, and 37 other countries around the world. Within the United States, Canada, New Zealand, Japan, Jamaica, and Singapore, ARMA has nearly 150 local chapters that provide networking and leadership opportunities through monthly meetings and special seminars.

ARMA's mission is to provide education, research, and networking opportunities to information professionals, to enable them to use their skills and experience to leverage the value of records, information, and knowledge as corporate assets and as contributors to organizational success.

The ARMA International headquarters office is located in Lenexa, Kansas, in the Kansas City metropolitan area. Office hours are 8:30 A.M. to 5:00 P.M., Central Time, Monday through Friday.

ARMA International
13725 W. 109th St., Ste. 101
Lenexa, Kansas 66215
800.422.2762 • 913.341.3808
Fax: 913.341.3742
hq@arma.org
www.arma.org